Zagreb Travel Guide 2024

Discovering Croatia's Hidden Gem: From the Upper Town to the Lower Town

By

Coast Walker Oz

Copyright © 2023 Coast Walker Oz

All rights reserved.

Contents

Introduction — 7
  Why Visit Zagreb — 10
  Planning Your Trip — 12

Chapter 1 — 18
  Getting to Know Zagreb — 18
    Zagreb's History — 19
    Geographical Overview — 22
    Local Culture and Traditions — 24
    Language and Communication — 27
    Travel Etiquette — 28

Chapter 2 — 31
  Navigating Zagreb — 31
    Getting Around the City — 31
    City Layout and Neighborhoods — 36

Chapter 3 — 44
  Where to Stay — 44
    Hotels — 44
    Bed and Breakfasts — 51
    Hostels and Guesthouses — 52
    Unique Lodging Options — 53

Chapter 4 — 55

Zagreb's Culinary Delights	55
Traditional Croatian Cuisine	55
Must-Try Dishes	60
Dining Etiquette	64
Cafes and Patisseries	67
Restaurants and Dining Recommendations	69
Chapter 5	**74**
Exploring Zagreb's Attractions	74
Museums and Galleries	74
Historic Landmarks	80
Hidden Gems and Local Secrets	87
Chapter 6	**90**
Arts and Culture in Zagreb	90
Zagreb's Art Scene	91
Zagreb Museum of Contemporary Art	92
Performing Arts	96
Cultural Festivals and Events	100
Chapter 7	**103**
Shopping in Zagreb	103
Souvenirs and Gifts	103
Markets and Flea Markets	107
Boutiques and Fashion	111

Antique Stores	112
Chapter 8	**115**
Day Trips and Excursions	115
Zagreb's Surroundings	116
Castles and Historic Sites	121
Natural Beauty and Adventure	122
Chapter 9	**127**
Practical Information	127
Safety and Emergency Contacts	128
Health and Medical Services	130
Money and Currency Exchange	131
Communication and Internet	133
Travel Tips and Packing Suggestions	134
Chapter 10	**137**
Zagreb for Different Travelers	137
Family-Friendly Zagreb	137
Romantic Getaways	140
Accessible Travel	144
Conclusion	**147**
Reflecting on Your Zagreb Experience	147
Farewell to Local Friends	148
Last-Minute Explorations	149

A Last Taste of Zagreb's Cuisine 151
Leaving a Positive Impact 152
Farewell, but Not Goodbye 154
Zagreb Travel Journal **155**

Introduction

Welcome to Zagreb, the enchanting capital of Croatia and one of Europe's best-kept secrets. Situated northwest of the country, this vibrant city combines a rich historical heritage with a modern, cosmopolitan atmosphere. Zagreb has something to offer to every traveler, whether you're a history buff, a foodie, an art enthusiast, or seeking unique experiences off the beaten path.

Zagreb is often described as a city of contrasts. It's a

place where centuries-old architecture and cobbled streets meet contemporary art and lively street culture. The city's distinctive dual character splits it into two parts - the Upper Town (Gornji Grad) and the Lower Town (Donji Grad), each with its unique charm and character.

Upper Town

In the Upper Town, you'll find well-preserved historic buildings, charming cafes, and an old-world atmosphere that transports you back in time. Meanwhile, the Lower Town is a bustling hub of modern life, filled with trendy restaurants, museums, and vibrant parks. Zagreb seamlessly bridges the gap between tradition and modernity, allowing travelers to experience the best of both worlds.

Whether you're strolling through the historic streets of the Old Town or indulging in a rich culinary adventure, Zagreb's warmth and welcoming spirit are ever-present. The locals are known for their hospitality, and it's not uncommon to have a friendly conversation with a stranger at a café or market.

This travel guide will take you on a journey through Zagreb's most captivating attractions, guide you on where to stay, help you explore the city's culinary delights, and offer insight into the city's cultural scene. Whether you're a solo traveler, a family, a romantic couple, or someone with specific interests, Zagreb has a treasure trove of experiences waiting for you.

Why Visit Zagreb

You might wonder why you should choose Zagreb as your next travel destination. Here are some compelling reasons to visit this remarkable city:

Rich History: Zagreb's history dates back to Roman times, and you'll find traces of this heritage in ancient architecture, churches, and museums. The city's historical charm is beautifully preserved, making it a treasure trove for history enthusiasts.

Cultural Delights: Zagreb is a vibrant cultural hub with numerous museums, galleries, theaters, and festivals celebrating art in all its forms. You can explore everything from contemporary art to classical music in this city.

Food and Wine: Croatian cuisine is a hidden gem, and Zagreb is a fantastic place to indulge in culinary delights. The city's culinary scene is a culinary adventure from traditional dishes like "štrukli" and "čevapi" to modern, fusion cuisine.

Natural Beauty: Surrounded by hills and forests, Zagreb offers a green escape within the city limits. Parks and recreational areas are ideal for a leisurely walk, a picnic, or a hike.

Affordability: Zagreb is one of the more budget-friendly destinations in Europe. You can enjoy a high-quality experience without breaking the bank, from affordable accommodation to reasonably priced meals and activities.

Festivals and Events: The city hosts various festivals and events yearly. The Zagreb Film Festival, INmusic Festival, and Advent in Zagreb are just a few examples of the vibrant cultural calendar.

Gateway to Croatia: Zagreb is an excellent starting point for exploring the rest of Croatia. Whether you want to venture to the coast, explore national parks, or visit other historic cities, Zagreb is well-connected and offers a central location for your Croatian adventure.

Planning Your Trip

When planning your trip to Zagreb, it's essential to consider various factors to ensure a smooth and enjoyable visit.

Best Time to Visit

Zagreb experiences four distinct seasons, and the best time to visit depends on your preferences and interests:

Spring (March-May): Spring brings mild temperatures and blossoming landscapes. It's an excellent time for outdoor activities, and you'll enjoy the city's lush greenery.

Summer (June - August): Summer is the peak tourist season when Zagreb comes alive with outdoor festivals and events. Expect warm weather but also larger crowds and higher prices.

Autumn (September - November): This is a lovely time to visit as the weather remains pleasant, and you'll find fewer tourists. The changing colors of the trees create a picturesque backdrop.

Winter (December - February): Zagreb's Advent season is a magical experience with Christmas markets, ice skating, and holiday lights. If you're a fan of winter activities, this is the time to visit.

Duration of Stay

The ideal duration of your Stay in Zagreb largely depends on your interests and the depth of exploration you desire. Here are some general recommendations:

Short Stay (2-3 Days): A short stay is perfect for quickly introducing the city. You can explore the major attractions, sample the local cuisine, and enjoy the city's ambiance.

Medium Stay (4-6 Days): With a medium stay, you can dive deeper into Zagreb's cultural scene, visit museums and galleries, and take day trips to nearby attractions.

Extended Stay (7+ Days): An extended stay allows you to immerse yourself in the city's culture, explore surrounding regions, and discover hidden gems. It's also ideal if you want to attend multiple festivals or events.

Budget Planning

Zagreb is considered a budget-friendly destination in Europe, making it an excellent choice for travelers who want to get the most value for their money. Here are some key budget planning considerations:

Accommodation: Zagreb offers a range of accommodation options, from luxury hotels to budget hostels and guesthouses. Prices vary significantly, so research and book in advance to secure the best deals.

Food: Dining in Zagreb is relatively affordable, especially if you choose local restaurants and cafes over upscale dining establishments. Street food and markets also offer budget-friendly meal options.

Transportation: Public transportation in Zagreb is efficient and reasonably priced. Consider buying a

Zagreb Card for unlimited travel on trams and buses and discounts at museums and attractions.

Activities and Attractions: Many of Zagreb's attractions are free or have modest entrance fees. Plan your itinerary to include a mix of paid and free activities.

Shopping: Set aside a shopping budget if you plan to purchase souvenirs or unique local products. Zagreb's markets and boutiques offer a wide range of shopping opportunities.

Visa and Entry Requirements

As of my last knowledge update in September 2021, Croatia is part of the European Union (EU), and the entry requirements may vary depending on your citizenship and the purpose of your visit.

You must check the most up-to-date visa and entry requirements with the Croatian embassy or consulate in your home country and ensure you have the necessary travel documents before your trip. Here are some general guidelines:

EU and EEA Citizens: If you are a citizen of an EU or European Economic Area (EEA) country, you typically do not need a visa to enter Croatia for tourism or short visits. A valid passport or national ID card is sufficient.

Non-EU/EEA Citizens: Citizens of non-EU/EEA countries may require a visa to enter Croatia for tourism. Visa requirements vary, so check with your home country's Croatian embassy or consulate for specific details and application procedures.

Schengen Zone: Croatia is not part of the Schengen Area, so if you plan to visit other Schengen countries during your trip, be aware that you might need separate visas or travel documents for those countries.

Passport Validity: Ensure your passport is valid for at least six months beyond your departure date from Croatia.

Please note that entry requirements can change, so it's essential to stay updated and consult the official

Croatian government website or your country's embassy or consulate for the latest information.

Zagreb is a captivating destination with a rich history, vibrant culture, and culinary delights. By considering the best time to visit, the duration of your stay, budget planning, and visa requirements, you can prepare for an unforgettable journey to this unique European city.

As you continue reading this guide, you'll gain a deeper understanding of what makes Zagreb a must-visit destination and discover its best experiences.

Chapter 1

Getting to Know Zagreb

From its ancient beginnings to its contemporary identity, Zagreb's fascinating journey through time depicts a city firmly anchored in the past while embracing the present and future.

Zagreb city view

The geographical overview showcases how Zagreb's location between the Sava River and Medvednica Mountain shapes its character and climate. Discovering local culture and traditions, including folk festivals and coffee culture, will help travelers engage with the city's soul. Understanding language and communication is vital for seamless interactions with locals while adhering to travel etiquette ensures a respectful and rewarding visit to this vibrant Croatian gem. In this exploration, we set the stage for an in-depth adventure into the heart of Zagreb.

Zagreb's History

Zagreb, the capital city of Croatia, is where history comes to life. The city's roots trace back to Roman times, but it truly began to take shape in the Middle Ages. Zagreb's rich and complex history has left an indelible mark on its culture and character.

Ancient Origins

The area around present-day Zagreb has been inhabited for thousands of years. In Roman times, the city was known as Andautonia and was an important trade and military center. The remnants of Roman heritage can still be seen in the city, particularly in the form of archeological sites.

The Medieval Era

The medieval period saw the emergence of two distinct towns on either side of the Sava River. Gradec, on the hill, and Kaptol, in the valley, were two separate settlements that eventually merged to become Zagreb. The 13th century is considered the official birth of the city. The Church of St. Mark in Gradec and Zagreb Cathedral in Kaptol still stand as iconic symbols of this period.

Habsburg Influence

The Habsburgs played a significant role in shaping Zagreb's history, as with much of Central Europe. In the 18th century, Zagreb became the center of political and administrative power for the Kingdom of Croatia within the Habsburg Monarchy. Establishing the Ban's Office (Banovina) in Zagreb marked the city's prominence.

The Twentieth Century

In the 20th century, she brought a series of transformative events to Zagreb. After World War I, Zagreb became the capital of the Kingdom of Yugoslavia. During World War II, the city experienced significant hardships under Nazi occupation. Post-war, Zagreb became the capital of the Socialist Republic of Croatia, part of the former Yugoslavia. The 1990s marked the city's shift toward modernity with the breakup of Yugoslavia and Croatia's declaration of independence.

Zagreb Today

Zagreb, as the capital of an independent Croatia, has continued to evolve. Its rich history is visible in the architecture, museums, and traditions passed down through generations. From the vibrant street life of Tkalciceva Street to the solemn beauty of the Zagreb Cathedral, the city's history is palpable in its every nook and cranny.

Geographical Overview

Zagreb's geographical location is crucial in shaping the city's character. Nestled in the northwest of Croatia, it sits at the foot of the Medvednica Mountain, along the banks of the Sava River. This unique position influences the city's climate, scenery, and lifestyle.

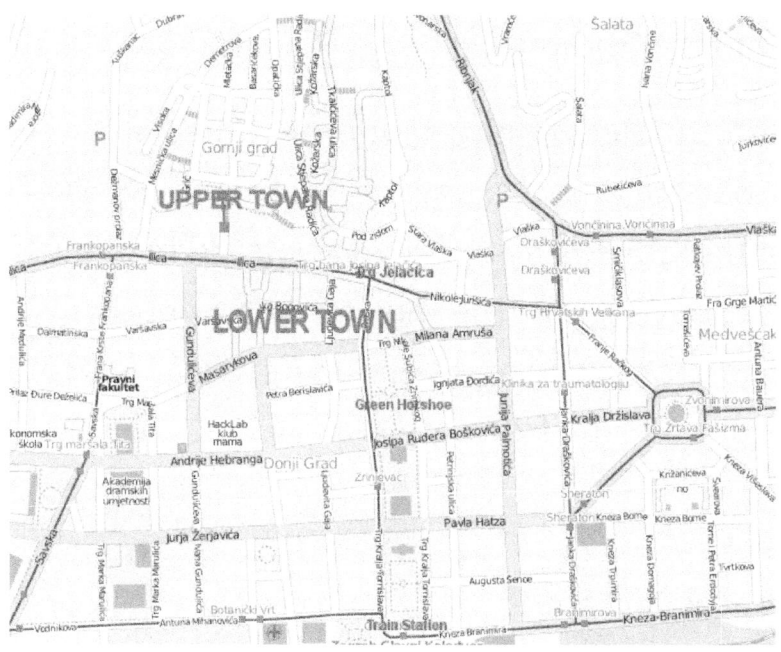

Zagreb's city map

The Sava River

The Sava River divides the city into the northern Novi Zagreb and the older, southern part of the city. While the Sava has often been a challenging neighbor due to its tendency to flood, it also provides scenic beauty and opportunities for recreation. The riverbanks are a popular destination for walking, cycling, and picnicking.

Medvednica Mountain

To the north, Medvednica Mountain offers a striking backdrop to the city. At its summit, Sljeme, you can find the Sljeme TV tower and the medieval fortress Medvedgrad. The mountain is a popular destination for hiking and skiing, offering a picturesque escape from city life.

Continental Climate

Zagreb experiences a continental climate characterized by distinct seasons. Winters can be cold with snowfall, while summers are warm and often quite pleasant. The transition between seasons brings colorful foliage in the fall and vibrant blooms in the spring.

Local Culture and Traditions

Understanding the local culture and traditions is critical to immersing yourself in the Zagreb experience. The city's culture is deeply rooted in its history and celebrated through various customs and events.

Folklore and Festivals

Croatian folklore plays a vital role in the city's cultural landscape. Folk music, dance, and costumes are integral to Zagreb's traditions. You can experience this rich heritage during various festivals and events, including the annual International Folklore Festival in Zagreb.

Outdoor Markets

Zagreb's outdoor markets are places to shop and cultural landmarks. Dolac, the central market, is where locals gather to buy fresh produce, flowers, and handmade crafts. It's a perfect place to witness the daily rhythm of life in the city.

Advent in Zagreb

One of the most beloved traditions in Zagreb is "Advent u Zagrebu," or Advent in Zagreb. It's a month-long celebration leading up to Christmas.

The city transforms into a winter wonderland with festive decorations, open-air concerts, and various food and craft stalls.

Coffee Culture

Croatians take their coffee seriously, and Zagreb is no exception. The coffee culture in the city is deeply ingrained in daily life. Local cafes are social hubs where people slowly gather to chat, read, or savor their coffee. It's customary to sit and linger over coffee, enjoying the company of friends or a good book.

St. Blaise's Day

St. Blaise's Day, celebrated on February 3rd, is an essential religious and cultural holiday in Zagreb. The city's cathedral, dedicated to St. Blaise, hosts a special mass. A procession through the city follows, led by a statue of St. Blaise.

Language and Communication

The primary language spoken in Zagreb is Croatian. However, in the city center and tourist areas, you'll find that many people speak English, especially in restaurants, hotels, and shops. Learning a few basic Croatian phrases can be helpful and is appreciated by the locals.

Basic Phrases

"Hello" - "Bok" (pronounced "bohk")

"Please" - "Molim" (pronounced "moh-leem")

"Thank you" - "Hvala" (pronounced "hvah-lah")

"Yes" - "Da" (pronounced "dah")

"No" - "Ne" (pronounced "neh")

"Excuse me" - "Izvinite" (pronounced "eez-vee-nee-teh")

Non-Verbal Communication

Croatians are generally warm and welcoming, but there are some unspoken rules of etiquette. Greeting with a handshake is customary, and a slight nod is considered polite. When in doubt, it's always safe to be respectful and friendly.

Travel Etiquette

Travel etiquette in Zagreb follows standard international norms, but understanding local customs and behaviors will help you make a positive impression and enjoy your visit to the fullest.

Tipping

Tipping is customary in Zagreb. Leaving a tip of 10-15% of the bill is standard in restaurants, although rounding up the bill is also appreciated. In cafes, you can go for small change, and in taxis, rounding up is common.

Dress Code

Zagreb is a relatively casual city, but when visiting churches, cathedrals, and upscale restaurants, it's advisable to dress modestly. Revealing clothing is not suitable in such locations. Comfortable shoes for exploring the city's historic streets and parks are necessary.

Public Behavior

Public behavior is generally respectful in Zagreb. It's customary to wait your turn in lines, give up your seat for the elderly or disabled on public transportation, and keep noise levels down in residential areas during the evening.

Photography

When taking photos, it's best to ask for permission if you plan to photograph people, especially in more intimate settings. Respect "no photography" signs in museums and churches. Most public places, however, are open for photography.

Understanding Zagreb's history, geography, culture, language, and travel etiquette is essential to making the most of your visit. With this foundation, you can dive deeper into the city's unique charm, explore its historic sites, and connect with its friendly locals. Zagreb's stories and traditions await you, offering a vibrant and authentic experience in the heart of Croatia.

Chapter 2

Navigating Zagreb

Navigating Zagreb is an essential aspect of any visit to the capital of Croatia. The city, with its rich history and diverse neighborhoods, offers many experiences for travelers. In this chapter, we will delve into the various ways to get around Zagreb, explore its layout and communities, understand the importance of maps and wayfinding, and discover the invaluable role of tourist information centers.

Getting Around the City
Zagreb is a city that combines the charm of a European metropolis with the intimacy of a small town, making it relatively easy to explore. The transportation choice depends on your preferences and the areas you want to visit. Here are the primary modes of getting around Zagreb:

Public Transportation

Zagreb boasts an efficient and well-connected public transportation system, which includes trams, buses, and a funicular. The city's tram network is extensive, covering almost every corner of Zagreb. Trams are popular with locals and tourists due to their convenience and affordability. The trams are easy to spot with their distinctive blue and yellow color scheme.

Tips for using public transportation

ZET Tickets: Tickets for trams and buses can be purchased at kiosks, newsstands, or through ticket vending machines at tram stops. Buying a Zagreb Card is advisable, which provides unlimited travel on trams and buses for a specified duration.

Tram Numbers: Each tram route is identified by a number, and the way is displayed on the front. Be sure to check the number and directions before boarding.

Timetables: Trams generally run from early morning to midnight, with reduced weekend service. Check the timetable in advance to avoid any inconvenience.

Funicular: The Zagreb Funicular is one of the shortest funiculars in the world and connects the Lower Town (Donji Grad) to the Upper Town (Gornji Grad). It's a unique and fun way to traverse the hilly terrain.

Taxis and Ride-Sharing

Taxis are readily available in Zagreb, and ride-sharing services like Uber have also gained popularity. Taxis are regulated and generally safe, but it's advisable to use licensed taxis. You can identify them by the taxi sign on the roof and a displayed fare chart inside. Be sure to ask for a receipt after your ride.

Ride-sharing services like Uber offer the convenience of booking a ride through a mobile app. This option is often preferred by travelers who want to know the fare in advance and have a record of their driver's information.

Tips for taxis and ride-sharing

Language: Most taxi drivers in Zagreb speak limited English, so having your destination written down or marked on a map is a good idea.

Pricing: Taxis in Zagreb generally have a start fee, followed by a per-kilometer rate. Be aware of the standard pricing and any extra costs for luggage or late-night rides.

Uber: If you prefer ride-sharing, ensure you have the app installed on your smartphone and are familiar with booking a ride.

Walking and Biking

Zagreb's compact city center makes it a delightful place for pedestrians. Walking is one of the best ways to explore the city's charming streets, parks, and historic sites. Many of the city's attractions are within walking distance of each other, especially in the Upper and Lower Towns.

For those who enjoy biking, Zagreb has made efforts to become a more bike-friendly city. Bike lanes and bike-sharing programs are available, allowing you to rent bicycles for short periods. Exploring the city on two wheels can be a unique and eco-friendly experience.

Tips for walking and biking

Comfortable Shoes: Wear comfortable walking shoes as you'll likely do much exploring on foot.

Safety: Follow pedestrian rules and use designated bike lanes when cycling. Helmets are not required but are recommended for protection.

Bike Rentals: Look for bike rental stations or inquire about renting a bike for the day at your accommodation.

City Layout and Neighborhoods

Understanding Zagreb's layout and neighborhoods is crucial for an enriching travel experience. The city is divided into several districts, each with its unique character. Here are some of the critical areas to explore:

Upper Town (Gornji Grad)

The Upper Town is the historical heart of Zagreb and is known for its old-world charm. This area is home to many of the city's iconic landmarks, including St. Mark's Church, Lotrščak Tower, and the Croatian Parliament.

Zagreb Upper Town

Cobblestone streets, quaint squares, and colorful buildings give the Upper Town a fairytale-like ambiance.

Highlights of the Upper Town

St. Mark's Square: A picturesque square with St. Mark's Church, known for its colorful tiled roof depicting the coat of arms of Zagreb and Croatia.

Lotrščak Tower: Climb this historic tower for panoramic views of the city and witness the daily firing of the cannon, the Gric Cannon, at noon.

Museums: Explore museums like the Museum of Broken Relationships and the Zagreb City Museum.

Lower Town (Donji Grad)

The Lower Town, characterized by its superb 19th-century architecture, is Zagreb's economic and commercial center. You'll find bustling streets, shops, restaurants, and cultural institutions here. It's great for shopping, dining, and experiencing Zagreb's contemporary lifestyle.

Highlights of the Lower Town

Ban Jelačić Square: The central square and a gathering point for locals and tourists, named after the iconic Ban Josip Jelačić.

Art Pavilion and King Tomislav Square: Admire the beautiful art pavilion and relax in the peaceful King Tomislav Square.

Zrinjevac Park: A picturesque park with fountains, greenery, and open-air events.

Other Districts

Beyond the Upper and Lower Towns, Zagreb has several other districts worth exploring. Novi Zagreb is a newer area with modern architecture and a more suburban feel, while Jarun is known for its lakeside recreational activities. The Maksimir Park area is perfect for nature lovers, with a vast park and the Zagreb Zoo.

Maps and Wayfinding

While Zagreb is generally easy to navigate, having maps and wayfinding tools can be immensely helpful, especially when exploring lesser-known neighborhoods or finding specific points of interest. Here are some resources to aid you in your navigation:

Tourist Maps: You can obtain free tourist maps at information centers hotels, or download digital versions from official tourism websites. These maps often include marked attractions, public transportation routes, and valuable tips.

Smartphone Apps: Various smartphone apps, such as Google Maps and local navigation apps, can help you find your way around Zagreb. Download offline maps to avoid data charges while exploring.

Street Signs: Zagreb has well-labeled street signs, making it easy to find your way around. Street names are typically displayed in both Croatian and English.

Tourist Signage: Throughout the city, you'll find signs pointing you to major attractions, museums, and landmarks. These directional signs are beneficial for pedestrians.

Tourist Information Centers

Tourist information centers are valuable resources for travelers, providing information, assistance, and local insights. In Zagreb, these centers are conveniently located in various parts of the city, including the central train station and critical tourist districts. The staff at these centers are typically multilingual and eager to help you make the most of your visit.

Services provided by tourist information centers:

Maps and Brochures: Pick up maps, brochures, and guides to the city's attractions and events.

Transportation Assistance: Get help with public transportation schedules, ticket information, and directions to specific locations.

Accommodation Recommendations: Staff can advise on finding suitable accommodations based on your preferences and budget.

Event Information: Learn about local festivals, exhibitions, and events during your visit.

Language Assistance: If you encounter language barriers, the staff can assist in translating or providing written directions.

In conclusion, navigating Zagreb is an integral part of your travel experience. Whether you explore the city by tram, taxi, on foot, or by bike, you'll find it relatively straightforward to get around. Understanding the layout of the Upper and Lower Towns and other districts will help you make the most of your time in this captivating city. Additionally, maps, wayfinding tools, and the assistance of tourist information centers ensure that you can confidently explore Zagreb and make the most of your visit.

Chapter 3

Where to Stay

When planning a trip to Zagreb, one of the most important aspects to consider is your choice of accommodation. The city offers a wide range of lodging options, catering to all travelers and budgets. In this chapter, we will explore the various places to stay in Zagreb, from luxurious hotels to charming bed and breakfasts, budget accommodations, hostels, guesthouses, and unique lodging options.

Hotels
Hotels in Zagreb are abundant and diverse, making it relatively easy to find one that suits your preferences and budget. Whether you seek the utmost luxury or a more budget-friendly option, Zagreb's hotels have something for everyone.

Luxury Hotels

Zagreb boasts an array of luxury hotels that provide an unforgettable experience for travelers seeking the pinnacle of comfort and service. Here are a few of the most renowned luxury hotels in the city:

Esplanade Zagreb Hotel: This iconic five-star hotel is a historical gem near the central train station.

The Esplanade offers opulent rooms, exquisite dining, and an old-world charm that transports you back in time. It's a favorite among celebrities and dignitaries visiting Zagreb.

The Westin Zagreb: This upscale hotel offers elegance and sophistication in the city's heart. The Westin features spacious rooms, exceptional dining options, and a wellness center with a fantastic view of Zagreb.

Sheraton Zagreb Hotel: Situated near the city center, the Sheraton offers luxurious rooms, excellent meeting facilities, and a tranquil atmosphere.

The hotel is perfect for both business and leisure travelers.

Mid-Range Hotels

Mid-range hotels in Zagreb provide a comfortable and affordable option for travelers who desire quality accommodation without extravagant costs. Here are some notable mid-range hotels:

Hotel Jägerhorn: Situated in the city center, this charming boutique hotel is one of Zagreb's oldest, offering a unique blend of modern amenities and historical character.

It's a favorite among budget-conscious travelers looking for consistency and convenience.

Hotel Academia: Nestled in the heart of the city, Hotel Academia offers well-appointed rooms and easy access to Zagreb's attractions, making it a popular choice for tourists.

Hotel Academia

Hotel Astoria: Located near the main square, Hotel Astoria combines comfort and affordability. It's a classic and welcoming hotel with a history dating back to the early 20th century.

Hotel Astoria

Hotel International: This mid-range hotel offers comfortable rooms and excellent business and leisure traveler facilities. It's known for its great value and central location.

Budget Accommodations

Travelers on a tight budget can find several budget accommodations in Zagreb, ranging from hostels to guesthouses and smaller hotels. These options provide a comfortable and cost-effective place to rest while exploring the city.

Hostel Shappy: This vibrant hostel is a favorite among backpackers and budget travelers. It offers dormitory-style and private rooms, a friendly atmosphere, and a central location.

Funk Lounge Hostel: Known for its lively atmosphere and social events, it is perfect for solo travelers looking to meet others. The hostel offers affordable dormitory and private rooms.

Hotel I: Located near the bus station, Hotel I provides budget-friendly accommodation with clean and comfortable rooms. It's an excellent choice for travelers in transit.

Swanky Mint Hostel: This trendy hostel offers a mix of dorms and private rooms. It's famous for its vibrant atmosphere, rooftop terrace, and great location in the heart of Zagreb.

These are just a few examples of the various hotels you can choose from when visiting Zagreb.

Depending on your preferences and budget, you'll find a wide range of options, making it possible to experience the city's charm and culture while staying within your comfort zone.

Bed and Breakfasts

Bed and breakfasts in Zagreb offer travelers a more intimate and personalized experience. They are often situated in charming residential neighborhoods, providing a homely atmosphere.

4City Windows: Located near the city center, this B&B offers cozy rooms with a homey feel. The hosts are known for their warm hospitality and delicious breakfasts.

Prestige Apartments Zagreb: If you want a blend of modern comfort and a personalized touch, this B&B is an excellent choice. It provides well-furnished apartments in a peaceful neighborhood.

Kaptol Hostel Bed & Breakfast: This budget-friendly B&B offers a variety of room options and a central location. It's perfect for travelers seeking affordable yet comfortable accommodation.

Hostels and Guesthouses

Hostels and guesthouses in Zagreb are great options for budget-conscious travelers and those seeking a more social environment.

Main Square Hostel: As its name suggests, it is located on Ban Jelačić Square. It's famous for its prime location and lively atmosphere, making it an excellent choice for social travelers.

Hostel Bureau: Situated in the heart of Zagreb, Hostel Bureau offers a comfortable and affordable place to stay. It's known for its friendly staff and communal areas.

Guesthouse Lessi: If you prefer a guesthouse over a hostel, Guesthouse Lessi is a charming choice. It provides clean and cozy rooms and a warm atmosphere, making guests feel like they're staying with friends.

Unique Lodging Options

Some unique lodging options are available for travelers seeking a one-of-a-kind experience in Zagreb.

Hotel Le Premier: This boutique hotel combines luxury with unique art and design. Each room is decorated by a different artist, making it a fascinating and artistic place to stay.

Zagreb 360°: If you want a room with a view, the Zagreb 360° offers panoramic views of the city from its upper floors. It's a perfect choice for those who appreciate breathtaking vistas.

The Movie Hotel: Film enthusiasts will love The Movie Hotel, which is dedicated to the world of cinema. Each room has a different movie theme, providing an unusual and fun lodging experience.

Hostel Swanky Hostel: This unique hostel offers a treehouse vibe with its wooden interior and themed rooms. It's a playful and unconventional place to stay in the heart of Zagreb.

In conclusion, when finding a place to stay in Zagreb, you have many options catering to every taste and budget. Whether you prefer the luxury and opulence of high-end hotels, the cozy and personal touch of bed and breakfasts, the social atmosphere of hostels and guesthouses, or the novelty of unique lodging options, Zagreb has something for everyone.

Regardless of your choice, you'll have the opportunity to experience the city's rich culture and explore its many attractions.

Chapter 4

Zagreb's Culinary Delights

Zagreb, the capital of Croatia, boasts a rich culinary tradition that reflects the country's diverse history and influences from Mediterranean, Central European, and Balkan cuisines.

This chapter will explore the mouthwatering world of Zagreb's culinary delights. From traditional Croatian dishes to dining etiquette and recommendations for cafes and restaurants, this section will guide you on a gastronomic journey through the city's heart.

Traditional Croatian Cuisine
Croatian cuisine is deeply rooted in tradition, and Zagreb serves as a melting pot for regional flavors and culinary heritage. Here are some elements of

traditional Croatian cuisine to savor while in Zagreb:

Ingredients

Croatian cuisine is characterized by the use of fresh, locally sourced ingredients. The country's diverse geography, with its pristine coastline, fertile plains, and lush forests, provides various components. Olive oil, wine, truffles, and a wide array of Mediterranean vegetables are staples along the coast, while continental Croatia offers hearty ingredients like pork, lamb, freshwater fish, and game.

Influences

Neighboring countries have influenced Croatian cuisine over the centuries. Central European cuisines, predominantly Hungarian and Austrian, have left their mark with goulash, schnitzel, and strudel. Mediterranean influences shine through in the coastal regions, with seafood, olive oil, and aromatic herbs playing a prominent role.

Dalmatian Cuisine

almatian (Mediterranean) cuisine

From the coastal region of Croatia, Dalmatian cuisine is known for its simplicity and emphasis on fresh, local ingredients. Grilled fish, seafood, octopus salads, and pasticada (marinated beef) are typical delights. Try 'peak,' a traditional way of cooking under a bell-like lid, which imparts a unique flavor to the dishes.

Continental Delicacies

You'll encounter heartier dishes in the continental part of Croatia, including Zagreb. 'Štrukli,' a baked or boiled pastry filled with cheese, is a Zagreb specialty. 'Zagorski štrukli' features a creamy cheese filling, making it a must-try in the city.

Pag Cheese

One culinary gem of Croatia is Pag cheese, produced on the island of Pag. This hard cheese has a distinct flavor thanks to the island's salty winds and unique vegetation. It pairs wonderfully with prosciutto and olives, creating a delightful appetizer.

Traditional Meats

Croatia, and by extension Zagreb, is known for its meat dishes. 'Ćevapi,' small minced meat sausages served with pita bread and onions, are a popular street food. 'Peka na žaru' features grilled meats, often served with 'ajvar,' a roasted red pepper and eggplant spread.

Wine and Spirits

Croatia boasts a burgeoning wine scene with numerous indigenous grape varieties. Be sure to taste the local wines, including Plavac Mali and Pošip, which have received international recognition. Regarding spirits, 'rakija' is a traditional fruit brandy, and 'Medica' is a honey liqueur, both enjoyed as aperitifs or digestifs.

Must-Try Dishes
In Zagreb, you'll have the opportunity to savor various dishes that capture the essence of Croatian

cuisine. Here are some must-try words that will make your culinary journey memorable:

Štrukli

As mentioned earlier, 'štrukli' is a beloved Zagreb dish. It's a unique blend of cottage cheese and baked or boiled dough. The result is a comforting, cheesy delight that showcases the region's flavors.

Peka

Peka is a traditional method of cooking that combines various ingredients, typically meat or seafood, with vegetables, herbs, and olive oil. The ingredients are slow-cooked under a bell-like lid, resulting in succulent and flavorful dishes. Peka can be found at many restaurants in Zagreb.

Crni Rižot (Black Risotto)

While you might not be on the coast in Zagreb, you can still indulge in Crni Rižot, a black risotto made with squid ink. It's a sumptuous dish showcasing

Mediterranean flavors' influence even in the heart of Croatia.

Crni Rižot

Kulen

Kulen is a spiced, fermented sausage specialty of the Slavonia region in Croatia. It's known for its bold flavors and makes for a fantastic appetizer or addition to a cheese platter.

Pašticada

Pašticada is a slow-cooked beef dish marinated in a sweet and sour sauce, typically served with gnocchi. It's a classic Croatian meal reflecting Venetian cuisine's influence on the region.

Paštikada

Dining Etiquette

Understanding dining etiquette in Zagreb and Croatia is essential for a pleasant culinary experience. Here are some dining customs and tips to keep in mind:

Tipping

Tipping is customary in Croatia, and it is expected to leave a tip of around 10% of the bill. However, check your account to ensure a service charge has not been included.

Punctuality

Croatians appreciate punctuality. If you have a reservation at a restaurant, make sure to arrive on time or a few minutes early.

Greetings

When entering a restaurant, it's polite to greet the staff with a simple "Dobar dan" (Good day) or "Dobra večer" (Good evening). "Hvala" (Thank you) is used to express gratitude.

Toasting

Croatians enjoy toasting, and it's customary to make eye contact and say "Živjeli!" (Cheers!) before taking a sip. When toasting, clinking glasses with everyone at the table is common.

Utensils

Eating utensils are used in Western dining customs. The fork is held in the left hand, and the knife in the right. When you've finished your meal, place your knife and fork parallel to each other on the plate to signal that you're done.

Dress Code

While Zagreb is a cosmopolitan city, some upscale restaurants may have a dress code. Checking the dress requirements before dining at a particular establishment is a good idea.

Cafes and Patisseries

Zagreb's cafe culture is vital to the city's social fabric. From enjoying a leisurely coffee to indulging in delectable pastries, here's what you need to know about cafes and patisseries in the city:

Coffee Culture

Coffee holds a special place in the hearts of Zagreb's residents. Numerous cafes are scattered throughout the city, each offering a unique atmosphere. Try the traditional Croatian coffee known as 'kava,' or opt for an espresso, cappuccino, or any other coffee variant you prefer.

Cvjetni Trg (Flower Square)

Cvjetni Trg, or Flower Square, is a picturesque spot in the city where you can find numerous cafes and patisseries. It's an ideal place to relax and people-watch while enjoying coffee and a sweet treat.

Cvjetni Trg

Dolac Market

Dolac Market is another excellent place to experience Zagreb's cafe culture. It's a vibrant market where you can enjoy a coffee amidst the hustle and bustle of locals shopping for fresh produce and local products.

Sweets and Pastries

Croatians have a sweet tooth; you can't visit Zagreb without trying their pastries. 'Krafne,' or filled doughnuts, are famous, as are 'palačinke,' thin crepes filled with various sweet fillings like jam or chocolate.

Restaurants and Dining Recommendations

Zagreb offers a diverse culinary scene with restaurants to suit every palate. Here are some dining recommendations, from traditional Croatian eateries to international cuisine:

Vinodol

Vinodol is a Zagreb institution serving traditional Croatian cuisine in an inviting, old-world setting. Try their 'štrukli' or 'pašticada' for an authentic taste of the city.

Dubravkin Put

Dubravkin Put offers a fusion of Mediterranean and continental cuisine in an elegant yet cozy atmosphere. The seafood dishes are a standout, and the wine selection is exceptional.

Dubravkin Put

Agava

For a contemporary twist on Croatian flavors, visit Agava. This restaurant offers a diverse menu focusing on fresh, local ingredients. Their terrace is a lovely spot to dine in the warmer months.

Mundoaka Street Food

Mundoaka Street Food offers a delightful mix of international flavors in the heart of Zagreb. Their menu changes frequently, featuring dishes worldwide, ensuring a unique experience with every visit.

Lari i Penati

Lari i Penati is a charming restaurant that combines traditional Croatian dishes and modern interpretations. Their attention to detail and flavors make it a must-visit for food enthusiasts.

Zagreb's culinary scene reflects its rich history and diverse influences. Traditional Croatian cuisine, must-try dishes, dining etiquette, cafes, and restaurant recommendations all play a significant role in the city's vibrant food culture.

Whether you're a foodie seeking new flavors or a traveler looking to immerse yourself in local traditions, Zagreb's culinary delights will leave a lasting impression on your palate and heart. Bon appétit!

Chapter 5

Exploring Zagreb's Attractions

Zagreb, the capital of Croatia, is a city that seamlessly combines its rich history with modernity, offering a wide array of attractions for visitors to explore. This chapter delves into the diverse interests you can discover in the city, ranging from museums and galleries to historic landmarks, parks, and hidden gems.

Museums and Galleries
Museum of Broken Relationships

The Museum of Broken Relationships is a truly unique and emotionally charged institution that has captured the hearts of many visitors worldwide. It was founded by Olinka Vištica and Dražen Grubišić, who came up with the idea for this museum after their breakup.

This innovative museum is a testament to the power of human emotions and connections, making it one of the most thought-provoking attractions in Zagreb.

Located in the Upper Town (Gornji Grad), the Museum of Broken Relationships showcases a collection of personal items donated by people from all over the globe. Each item on display is accompanied by a story that describes the relationship it represents. These stories range from romantic breakups to familial disputes, capturing the full spectrum of human relationships.

As you wander through the museum, you'll encounter a wide variety of objects, from traditional love letters and photographs to more unusual items like a single high-heeled shoe and an axe. The emotional intensity of these objects, coupled with the stories attached, makes the Museum of Broken Relationships a place of catharsis and reflection for many visitors.

Visitors often find themselves both moved and entertained by the stories and artifacts on display. The museum provides a profound look into the complex web of human relationships and emotions, making it a must-visit destination in Zagreb.

Croatian National Theatre

If you appreciate the performing arts, the Croatian National Theatre, or Hrvatsko narodno kazalište (HNK), is a cultural gem in the heart of Zagreb. Established in the late 19th century, this historic theater has been a cornerstone of Croatia's artistic heritage.

The HNK Zagreb is renowned for its impressive Neo-Baroque architecture and stunning interior, which are attractions. The theater hosts various performances, including opera, ballet, and drama. Whether you're a fan of classical works or contemporary productions, the Croatian National Theatre offers a diverse program to cater to all tastes.

Check the schedule and book tickets if you plan to attend a performance. The atmosphere within the theater is enchanting, and the quality of the productions is top-notch. Attending a show at HNK Zagreb is an opportunity to enjoy exceptional artistry and immerse yourself in the city's vibrant cultural scene.

Modern Gallery

For art enthusiasts, the Modern Gallery (Galerija suvremene umjetnosti) in Zagreb is a treasure trove of contemporary Croatian art. This gallery is home to an extensive collection of 19th and 20th-century

Croatian art, showcasing the nation's artistic evolution.

The Modern Gallery's collection includes works by renowned Croatian artists such as Ivan Meštrović, Vlaho Bukovac, and many more. You can explore various artistic styles, from academic and realism to modernism and abstraction.

The gallery is housed in a historic building constructed to serve as a stock exchange. Its grand architecture and the juxtaposition of contemporary art make for an intriguing experience. You can wander through the spacious halls, admire the diverse art pieces, and gain insight into Croatia's cultural heritage.

Visitors often find that the Modern Gallery provides an opportunity to learn about the country's history and culture through the lens of its artists. The exhibitions are thoughtfully curated and frequently rotated to showcase different aspects of Croatian art.

Historic Landmarks
St. Mark's Church

St. Mark's Church (Crkva sv. Marka) is one of Zagreb's most iconic and historic landmarks. This captivating church is located in St. Mark's Square, in the heart of the Upper Town. What sets it apart is its stunning and uniquely tiled roof, which displays the coats of arms of Zagreb and Croatia.

The church's history dates back to the 13th century and has undergone several architectural changes over the centuries. Its Gothic and Romanesque elements contribute to its distinctive appearance.

Visitors can explore the church's interior, which features beautiful frescoes, sculptures, and stained glass windows.

St. Mark's Church is also the site of important political events, including the inauguration of the Croatian President. As a result, it serves as a symbol of national identity and pride. Whether you're interested in history, architecture, or simply capturing an iconic image of Zagreb, St. Mark's Church is a must-visit attraction.

Lotrščak Tower

Lotrščak Tower is essential to Zagreb's historic skyline and offers a glimpse into the city's medieval past. The tower is a remnant of the old city fortifications located in the Upper Town. Climbing to the top of the building provides a breathtaking panoramic view of the city, making it a favorite spot for photographers and tourists.

tršcak Tower

One of the most distinctive features of Lotrščak Tower is its cannon, which is fired every day at noon. This tradition dates back to the 19th century when the gun served as a time signal for the city. Today, it's more of a ceremonial event, and the firing of the cannon attracts a crowd of onlookers.

The tower houses the Gric Cannon Museum, where you can learn about its history and its role in the city's defense. The exhibit includes historical artifacts, documents, and an in-depth exploration of the cannon-firing tradition.

Zagreb Cathedral

Zagreb Cathedral, or the Cathedral of the Assumption of the Blessed Virgin Mary, is an architectural masterpiece and one of the city's most important religious landmarks. The cathedral's towering spires are visible from many parts of Zagreb, and its significance goes beyond its impressive appearance.

The cathedral's origins trace back to the 11th century and has undergone several reconstructions and renovations over the centuries. The current

Neo-Gothic structure dates back to the late 19th century and is a testament to the city's resilience and faith.

Visitors are welcome to explore the cathedral's interior, which features stunning stained glass windows, altars, and religious artifacts. The cathedral's spires can be climbed for panoramic views of the city.

In addition to its religious significance, Zagreb Cathedral symbolizes Croatia's cultural and historical heritage. It's a place to appreciate the art, architecture, and spirituality that have shaped the city.

Parks and Outdoor Activities

Zagreb offers a pleasant mix of urban life and natural beauty, making it an excellent destination for those who appreciate the outdoors. The city is dotted with parks, green spaces, and opportunities for outdoor activities.

One of the most beloved green areas in Zagreb is **Maksimir Park.**

This expansive park is home to lush landscapes, walking paths, and a zoo. It's a fantastic place to escape the hustle and bustle of the city and enjoy some leisurely time in nature. Visitors often go for picnics, jog, or relax amidst the serene environment.

Jarun Lake is another popular outdoor destination, offering swimming, water sports, and sunbathing opportunities.

The lake is surrounded by a recreational area with cafes and restaurants, making it ideal for a day of fun and relaxation.

If you prefer a more active outdoor experience, consider hiking in Medvednica Nature Park, just a short drive from the city center. There are numerous trails and vantage points where you can soak in the natural beauty and serenity of the area.

Hidden Gems and Local Secrets

While Zagreb has its share of well-known attractions, part of the city's charm lies in its hidden gems and local secrets. These lesser-known spots can offer a more authentic and off-the-beaten-path experience for curious travelers.

One such hidden gem is the hidden Courtyards (Skriveni Vrtovi). Tucked away in the heart of the Upper Town, these courtyards are hidden behind unassuming entrances and offer a peaceful escape from the bustling streets. You can explore these charming and often overlooked city corners, which often host art exhibitions, concerts, and cultural events.

Zagreb's street art scene is another local secret that reveals the city's vibrant and creative side. The walls of the Lower Town feature numerous colorful and thought-provoking murals created by local and international artists. Take a stroll and watch for these artistic expressions, which can turn a simple walk into an urban art adventure.

For a unique culinary experience, consider visiting a local farmers' market, such as Dolac Market. While not entirely hidden, these markets offer a glimpse into the daily lives of Zagreb's residents. You can explore stalls filled with fresh produce, homemade products, and authentic Croatian cuisine. It's an excellent place to taste local delicacies and engage with the friendly market vendors.

As you explore Zagreb's hidden gems and local secrets, you'll discover the city's authentic character and the warmth of its people. Embrace the opportunity to go off the beaten path and create memorable experiences in this captivating European capital.

Zagreb's attractions are a testament to the city's rich history, artistic heritage, and seamless blend of old and new. From emotionally charged museums to iconic landmarks, beautiful parks, and hidden gems, Zagreb offers diverse experiences for every type of traveler.

Whether you're seeking cultural enrichment, historical insights, or simply a place to unwind, the attractions in Zagreb will leave a lasting impression on your journey through Croatia's vibrant capital.

Chapter 6

Arts and Culture in Zagreb

Zagreb, Croatia's capital and largest city, is a hub of historical and architectural wonders and a vibrant center of arts and culture. From art galleries showcasing local and international talents to lively streets adorned with captivating street art, Zagreb has something for every art enthusiast.

Additionally, the city is a cultural powerhouse with a thriving performing arts scene and a calendar filled with exciting cultural festivals and events. This chapter will delve into the heart of Zagreb's arts and culture scene to help you make the most of your visit.

Zagreb's Art Scene

Zagreb's art scene is a treasure trove for those seeking to explore the world of creativity. The city has a rich visual arts tradition, and you can witness this through its numerous art galleries, each offering a unique perspective on art and culture.

Art Galleries

Zagreb boasts an array of public and private art galleries, catering to a diverse range of artistic tastes. Here are some of the must-visit art galleries in the city:

Museum of Contemporary Art (Muzej suvremene umjetnosti): Located in the Novi Zagreb district, this museum is a true gem for contemporary art lovers. The impressive building is a work of art, and it houses an extensive collection of Croatian and international contemporary art, including paintings, sculptures, multimedia installations, and more.

Zagreb Museum of Contemporary Art

Croatian Association of Artists (HDLU): Situated in the heart of Zagreb, this institution is a historic center for Croatian artists. It hosts a series of rotating exhibitions featuring various contemporary art forms, including paintings, photography, and sculptures.

Croatian Association of Artists

Gliptoteka - Croatian Academy of Sciences and Arts: Gliptoteka is home to a remarkable collection of sculptures and statues, many of which are significant in the Croatian art world. It's an excellent place to explore the sculptural heritage of the region.

Lauba - People and Art House (Kuća ljudi i umjetnosti Lauba): This modern gallery in a converted military facility showcases contemporary art through exhibitions and installations. It hosts shows by established and emerging artists, providing a platform for new and experimental artistic expressions.

Gallery Klovićevi Dvori: Named after the renowned Croatian artist Juraj Klović, this gallery is housed in a beautifully preserved historic building near the Upper Town.

It features a wide range of art, including classical and modern works, and frequently hosts temporary exhibitions of national and international importance.

Street Art

While traditional art galleries are a cornerstone of the city's art scene, take advantage of the chance to explore Zagreb's thriving street art culture. The streets of Zagreb are adorned with vibrant, thought-provoking murals and graffiti, turning the city into an open-air art gallery.

Walk through neighborhoods like Špansko, Volovčica and the streets surrounding Savska Cesta to witness some of the most impressive street art pieces.

One of Zagreb's most famous street art landmarks is the colorful "Zagreb Eye" mural, located near Ban Jelačić Square. This piece perfectly captures the energy and creativity of the city. Local and international street artists' bright and imaginative works can be found on the sides of buildings, underpasses, and trams, adding a dynamic and ever-changing element to Zagreb's urban landscape.

If you want a deeper understanding of the street art culture in Zagreb, consider taking a guided street art tour. Knowledgeable guides will walk you through the history and stories behind the artworks, giving you insights into the artists and the local subculture.

Performing Arts

Zagreb's performing arts scene is rich in history and buzzing with contemporary vitality. The city is home to numerous theaters, and you can catch various performances, from classical plays to avant-garde productions.

Theaters and Performances

Croatian National Theatre (Hrvatsko narodno kazalište): Established in the 19th century, this theater is a cultural institution in Zagreb. It offers performances of opera, ballet, and drama. The stunning architecture of the building itself is worth a visit, even if you don't catch a show.

Gavella Drama Theatre (Drama Kazalište Gavella):

This theater is known for its diverse repertoire, including classical and modern dramas and experimental productions. It's housed in a beautiful, intimate venue, offering an immersive theater experience.

Zagreb Youth Theatre (Zagrebačko kazalište mladih): Catering to a younger and more experimental crowd, this theater focuses on contemporary and alternative theater. It often hosts plays that challenge traditional norms and encourage critical thinking.

Croatian Radio Television Concert Hall (Koncertna dvorana Vatroslav Lisinski): Lisinski Hall is the primary venue for classical music concerts in Zagreb. It hosts orchestral performances, chamber music, and various other yearly musical events.

Music and Nightlife

Zagreb's nightlife is vibrant, and music plays a significant role in its allure. The city offers a wide range of music venues and nightlife experiences to suit all tastes:

Jazz Clubs: Jazz lovers can head to clubs like "The Sax!" and "Jazz & Cabaret Club Kontesa" for live jazz performances and a cozy atmosphere.

Electronic Music: Zagreb has a thriving electronic music scene, and clubs like "Mocvara" and "Tvornica Kulture" are renowned for hosting electronic music events featuring local and international DJs.

Live Music: If you're into live rock or indie music, venues like "Boogaloo" and "Vintage Industrial Bar" often host local and international bands, making them great places to experience live music in Zagreb.

Café Culture: Many of the city's cafes offer live acoustic performances, allowing you to enjoy music in a more laid-back setting while sipping coffee or cocktails.

Late-Night Entertainment: For those seeking a vibrant nightlife scene, the streets of Tkalčićeva and Radićeva are lined with bars and clubs that stay open late into the night, making them perfect for partygoers.

Cultural Festivals and Events

Zagreb's cultural calendar is brimming with events and festivals, celebrating various aspects of the city's heritage and contemporary creativity. Here are some notable festivals and events you might want to consider when planning your visit:

Zagreb Film Festival: This annual film festival, held in the fall, showcases a selection of the best contemporary films from around the world. It's an excellent opportunity to catch independent and international movies in various genres.

INmusic Festival: A highlight for music lovers, this open-air music festival takes place in June on the shores of Jarun Lake. It features a diverse lineup of local and international bands and artists.

ZagrebDox: A documentary film festival, ZagrebDox is one of the region's most prominent documentary film events. It provides a platform for thought-provoking and innovative documentary storytelling.

Advent in Zagreb: During the holiday season, Zagreb transforms into a magical winter wonderland. The city's Advent celebration features beautifully decorated streets, outdoor markets, and numerous cultural events, including live music and theatrical performances.

Museum Night (Noć muzeja): This one-night event in January allows visitors to explore the city's museums and galleries free of charge, with extended opening hours and special exhibitions. It's a unique opportunity to dive into Zagreb's cultural heritage.

Cost is best Festival: This street festival takes place in May and combines various artistic performances, from theater and dance to music and street art, creating a lively and entertaining atmosphere in the city center.

Zagreb is a dynamic city that celebrates art and culture in all its forms. Zagreb has something to offer whether you're interested in visual art, theater, music, or cultural festivals.

Take your time to explore the city's art galleries, discover the stories behind its street art, attend captivating theater performances, and immerse yourself in its vibrant music and nightlife. With a calendar full of cultural festivals and events, you can plan your visit to coincide with one of Zagreb's many artistic celebrations, ensuring a truly enriching experience.

Chapter 7

Shopping in Zagreb

Shopping in Zagreb is a delightful experience that caters to a wide range of interests and preferences. From traditional souvenirs and gifts to exploring the city's vibrant marketplaces, upscale boutiques, and antique stores, this chapter will guide you through the diverse shopping opportunities in the Croatian capital.

Souvenirs and Gifts

When visiting Zagreb, you'll want to bring back a piece of Croatia. Souvenir shops are scattered throughout the city, offering an array of items that encapsulate the culture and heritage of the region.

Traditional Croatian Souvenirs

Licitar Hearts: These heart-shaped, red cookies are decorated with intricate designs and symbolize love and tradition in Croatia. They are often exchanged as gifts during special occasions.

Croatian Wine and Olive Oil: Croatia has a long history of winemaking, and you'll find a variety of high-quality wines from local vineyards. Croatian olive oil is also renowned for its taste and quality.

Lavender Products: Lavender fields are standard in Croatia, especially in the region of Dalmatia. You can find lavender-infused soaps, oils, and sachets, which make for fragrant and relaxing souvenirs.

Hand-Painted Ceramics: Croatian pottery and ceramics are exquisite. Look for hand-painted plates, bowls, and tiles often featuring intricate, traditional designs.

Traditional Croatian Jewelry: Filigree jewelry is a longstanding Croatian tradition. Look for intricate silver or gold jewelry, including earrings, necklaces, and bracelets.

Croatian Liqueurs: Rakija, a strong fruit brandy, is popular among locals and tourists. You can also find herbal liqueurs like Travarica.

Croatian Sweets: Sample and purchase local sweets, such as Paprenjaci (gingerbread cookies) and Bajadera, a delicious chocolate nougat confection.

Croatian Folklore Items: In Croatia, traditional costumes and items like neckties (cravats) originated. You can find beautifully crafted ties and other folkloric elements.

Where to Shop for Souvenirs

Tkalciceva Street: Lined with charming shops and boutiques, this street is great for picking up souvenirs, including Croatian arts and crafts.

Tkalciceva Street

St. Mark's Square: Nearby shops sell traditional Croatian crafts, making it a convenient location to pick up souvenirs after exploring the historic St. Mark's Church.

Ilica Street: Zagreb's main shopping street features a mix of international and local stores where you can find various souvenirs.

Croatian Design Shops: For unique and contemporary designs, visit boutiques like 'Made in

Zagreb,' which feature locally crafted jewelry, clothing, and home decor.

Markets and Flea Markets

Zagreb is known for its vibrant flea markets, where you can immerse yourself in local life and find various products, from fresh produce to vintage treasures.

Dolac Market

Dolac Market, located just steps from Ban Jelačić Square, is Zagreb's most famous and vibrant market. It's often called the "belly of Zagreb" because it focuses on fresh food. The market is divided into two levels: the lower level is dedicated to fresh produce, including fruits, vegetables, meats, and dairy, while the upper level is a treasure trove of stalls selling local products, flowers, and traditional Croatian souvenirs. The vivid red umbrellas and traditional stalls make Dolac Market a picturesque spot for both shopping and photography.

Britanski Trg (British Square) Antique Market

This is Zagreb's go-to spot for antique enthusiasts. Every Sunday, Britanski Trg hosts a flea market where antique dealers, collectors, and locals gather to sell various items, including vintage furniture, books, coins, and old family heirlooms. It's an excellent place to hunt for unique and historically significant finds.

Hrelić Flea Market

Hrelić is the largest flea market in Zagreb and offers diverse goods. Open on Sundays, it's a place where you can find everything from clothing, electronics, and second-hand items to collectibles and memorabilia. While not as picturesque as Britanski Trg, Hrelić is known for its eclectic offerings and the thrill of finding hidden treasures.

Vinyl and Vintage Markets

Zagreb has a growing scene of vintage and vinyl markets, such as the Sunday Vintage Market at Koturaška and the Vinylmania Market. These markets cater to collectors and enthusiasts, offering a variety of vintage clothing, accessories, records, and music memorabilia.

Zagreb Christmas Market

f you visit Zagreb during the holiday season, take advantage of the Zagreb Christmas Market. Voted as the best Christmas market in Europe multiple times, it's a magical place filled with festive decorations, local crafts, and a wide variety of traditional holiday foods and beverages.

Boutiques and Fashion

Zagreb has a burgeoning fashion scene with a range of boutique shops that cater to diverse tastes. Whether you're looking for high-end designer clothing, unique streetwear, or Croatian-made fashion, you'll find plenty of options.

Designer Boutiques

Zagreb has its fair share of high-end fashion boutiques featuring international and local designers. Places like the Croatia Flagship Store, which specializes in cravats, or Pms Design, known for elegant women's wear, showcase the city's fashion-forward side.

Tkalciceva Street

This picturesque street is a fashion hub with boutiques and concept stores offering trendy clothing, accessories, and lifestyle products. From bohemian chic to modern elegance, you can explore diverse styles in this area.

Fashion District

Zagreb's Lower Town, particularly around Frankopanska Street and Vlaška Street, is where you'll find numerous fashion boutiques, including Croatian and international brands. These shops cater to various budgets and styles, making it easy to discover the latest fashion trends or classic pieces for your wardrobe.

Local Designers and Concept Stores

If you're interested in supporting local talent, Zagreb has numerous concept stores like Monoconcept and Karaka, where you can find unique pieces created by Croatian designers. These stores often feature not only clothing but also home decor and accessories.

Antique Stores

Antique enthusiasts and collectors will find Zagreb a treasure trove of vintage and historical items. The city's antique stores offer a glimpse into Croatia's rich past.

Antikvarijat Knjiga i Slika

Situated in the heart of Zagreb, this antique shop specializes in rare books, vintage photographs, maps, and postcards. It's a perfect place for bibliophiles and history buffs.

Staro Selo Antiques

Located near Maksimir Park, this shop boasts diverse antique items, including furniture, paintings, and collectibles. It's a delightful place to explore for those interested in period pieces.

Ožujsko Antikvarijat

This charming antique store is known for its selection of vintage furniture, porcelain, and retro household items. It's a step back in time and offers a glimpse into the everyday life of past generations in Croatia.

Ljubomir Antiques

Situated in Zagreb's Upper Town, Ljubomir Antiques is renowned for its collection of antique watches, jewelry, and vintage items. It's a must-visit for those who appreciate the craftsmanship of bygone eras.

Shopping in Zagreb is a delightful journey through the city's rich cultural heritage and contemporary lifestyle. Whether you're looking for traditional souvenirs, exploring bustling markets, hunting for unique fashion pieces, or collecting antiques, Zagreb offers an array of shopping experiences to suit all tastes and interests.

Take your time to explore the city's shopping scene and uncover the hidden gems that will make your visit to Zagreb genuinely memorable.

Chapter 8
Day Trips and Excursions

Zagreb, the charming capital of Croatia, is a city of dynamic contrasts. While it offers a vibrant urban experience with its cultural treasures, historic sites, and bustling streets, its true magic lies in the secrets waiting to be discovered beyond its city limits. Chapter 8 of our travel guide is dedicated to these captivating day trips and excursions, taking you through the diverse landscapes and historic riches surrounding Zagreb.

Whether you're an avid outdoor enthusiast yearning for adventure, a history buff in search of medieval castles and tales of love and intrigue, or a nature lover seeking tranquil lakes, cascading waterfalls, and untouched wilderness, this chapter has something for everyone. From the allure of

Zagreb's immediate surroundings to the historical treasures tucked away in neighboring towns and the breathtaking natural beauty that Croatia is celebrated for, you'll find many experiences waiting to be explored.

Zagreb's Surroundings

One of the many allures of Zagreb is its strategic location, surrounded by stunning natural beauty and historic gems. In this chapter, we'll explore the various day trips and excursions you can undertake from the Croatian capital to discover the rich tapestry of experiences available in its vicinity.

Medvednica Mountain

Nestled just to the north of Zagreb, Medvednica Mountain is an outdoor enthusiast's paradise. This lush, forested mountain range offers an array of hiking trails for all levels of expertise. Among the most popular routes is the one leading to Sljeme, the highest peak in Medvednica, where you can enjoy panoramic views of Zagreb and its surroundings.

n the winter, Sljeme is also a popular destination for skiing and snowboarding.

For those interested in wildlife, Medvednica is home to various animal species, including foxes, deer, and occasional bears. You might spot some of these creatures during your hike if you're lucky. Additionally, educational trails help visitors learn about the local flora and fauna.

Samobor

A short drive west of Zagreb takes you to the picturesque town of Samobor. Known for its charming medieval architecture and serene atmosphere, Samobor is an ideal day trip destination.

The town's central square, Trg King Tomislav, has colorful buildings, quaint cafes, and artisan shops. Be sure to try a famous Samobor kremsnita, a delicious cream cake that is a local specialty.

The surrounding nature is equally captivating, with hiking trails leading to the Samobor Hills, which offer breathtaking views of the town and the surrounding countryside. If you visit during the summer, take a refreshing dip in the pools of the Samoborsko Opatije nature reserve.

Trakošćan Castle

Located approximately an hour's drive from Zagreb, Trakošćan Castle is a stunning medieval fortress on a hill overlooking a tranquil lake. The castle is a well-preserved historical treasure that allows you to step back in time and explore its rooms, collections, and beautifully landscaped gardens. The castle's interior is a veritable time capsule featuring antique furniture, artwork, and historical artifacts.

The castle's surroundings are equally enchanting. The lake at the base of the hill offers paddle boating and picnicking opportunities, making Trakošćan Castle an ideal spot for a romantic excursion or a family day out.

Varazdin

A little over an hour's drive to the north of Zagreb, Varazdin is often called "Little Vienna" for its baroque architecture and elegant streets. This charming town is rich in history and culture. The historic city center is a delight to explore, with its well-preserved architecture, cobblestone streets, and numerous museums. Be sure to visit the Varazdin Castle, one of the most iconic landmarks in the region.

Varazdin is also known for its annual Špancirfest, a vibrant street festival featuring music, art, and various forms of entertainment. If you can visit during this festival, you'll experience the town's lively and creative spirit.

Castles and Historic Sites

Croatia is known for its rich history and well-preserved historic sites; the areas surrounding Zagreb are no exception. Here are some of the most captivating castles and historic locations that make for fantastic day trips.

Veliki Tabor Castle

Veliki Tabor Castle, situated around an hour's drive from Zagreb, is a captivating medieval fortress with a dramatic history. It is known for its legends and tales of forbidden love, and visiting here feels like stepping into a fairy tale. The castle has been exceptionally well-preserved, allowing you to explore its inner chambers, courtyards, and defensive walls.

The castle also hosts various cultural events and exhibitions, adding a contemporary touch to its historical charm. While in the area, stroll around the picturesque village of Veliki Tabor to get a taste of traditional rural life.

Oršić Castle

About 45 minutes from Zagreb, you'll find Oršić Castle, a beautifully restored baroque palace surrounded by lush gardens. The castle, which dates back to the 18th century, was the former residence of the Oršić family and is now a museum. It provides a glimpse into the noble life of the time, with its opulent interiors, rich collections, and beautiful surroundings.

The castle is known for its annual "Evenings in Oršić Castle" event, during which it hosts classical music concerts and other cultural performances, offering visitors a unique blend of history and artistry.

Natural Beauty and Adventure
Croatia is renowned for its stunning natural landscapes; the regions surrounding Zagreb are no

exception. These day trips are perfect if you're a nature lover and adventure seeker.

Plitvice Lakes National Park

A two-hour drive from Zagreb takes you to the world-famous Plitvice Lakes National Park, a UNESCO World Heritage site and one of Europe's most stunning natural wonders. The park boasts cascading lakes and waterfalls, surrounded by lush forests and wildlife. Visitors can explore the park via a network of wooden walkways and hiking trails, allowing for up-close encounters with the pristine waters and abundant flora and fauna.

Plitvice Lakes is a year-round destination, offering a unique and breathtaking experience each season. Whether you visit in spring, with the blossoming of wildflowers, or in winter, when the waterfalls freeze, you're in for a memorable adventure in the heart of nature.

Žumberak and Samobor Hills Nature Park

Žumberak and Samobor Hills Nature Park, located less than an hour's drive from Zagreb, is a haven for hikers, nature enthusiasts, and those seeking a peaceful retreat. The park's rolling hills, pristine rivers, and dense forests create a serene and idyllic landscape.

Hiking trails of various difficulty levels crisscross the park, catering to beginners and seasoned trekkers. You can explore the local flora and fauna while breathing in the fresh mountain air. If you're interested in local culture, visit tiny villages throughout the park to discover traditional crafts and hospitality.

Mrežnica River

For a day of aquatic adventure, head to the Mrežnica River, about an hour and a half from Zagreb. This emerald-green river is renowned for its crystal-clear waters and abundance of cascading waterfalls. Visitors can engage in activities like rafting, canoeing, and swimming in the refreshing river pools.

The untouched natural beauty of the Mrežnica River makes it an ideal place to escape the hustle and bustle of the city and immerse yourself in the peaceful tranquility of nature.

Zagreb's surroundings offer an incredible array of day trip options, whether you're interested in historical exploration, natural beauty, or adventure. From the medieval castles that transport you to another era to the serene natural parks and rivers that allow you to reconnect with nature, these excursions provide a well-rounded experience for all travelers. Be sure to plan your day trips and tours from Zagreb to make the most of your visit to this vibrant and diverse region of Croatia.

Chapter 9
Practical Information

As you embark on your journey to explore the vibrant city of Zagreb, you must be equipped with practical information to ensure a smooth and enjoyable experience. This chapter is your guide to the practical aspects of your trip, focusing on your safety, health, and medical services, managing your finances, staying connected, and providing valuable travel tips and packing suggestions.

In the following sections, we'll delve into the nuances of navigating the city while keeping yourself safe and well, managing your finances effectively, and maintaining communication with your loved ones and the digital world. We'll also offer you expert advice on what to pack, what local customs to respect, and how to make the most of your time in Zagreb.

Whether you're a first-time traveler to Croatia or a seasoned adventurer, this chapter will provide essential insights and practical tips to enrich your experience and help you make the most of your visit to this enchanting European capital. So, let's start by ensuring your trip to Zagreb is memorable for all the right reasons.

Safety and Emergency Contacts

Ensuring your safety while traveling is paramount. Zagreb is considered a safe destination for tourists, but it's wise to be aware of potential risks and how to address them. Here are some essential safety tips and emergency contacts:

Safety Tips

General Precautions: As in any other city, exercise common sense when exploring Zagreb. Avoid poorly lit or secluded areas at night, and keep an eye on your belongings in crowded places.

Street Scams: While Zagreb is generally safe, be aware of pickpockets in crowded tourist areas. Keep your belongings secure, and be cautious of people approaching you with overly friendly or suspicious intentions.

Local Laws and Customs: Familiarize yourself with local laws and customs to avoid unintentionally breaking any rules. For example, public drinking is prohibited in many areas.

Emergency Services: The emergency services number in Croatia is 112, and this number will connect you to police, fire, and medical assistance.

Emergency Contacts

Police: In non-emergency situations where you need police assistance or have lost your belongings, call the local police at 192.

Medical Emergencies: For medical emergencies, dial 194 or head to the nearest hospital. Most healthcare professionals in Zagreb speak English and other languages.

Fire Department: Call 193 for fire emergencies.

Health and Medical Services

Zagreb has a well-developed healthcare system, and you can expect good medical care should you need it during your visit. Here's what you should know about health and medical services:

Medical Facilities

Hospitals: Zagreb has several hospitals and medical centers. The most prominent include the University Hospital Center Zagreb and Dubrava Clinical Hospital. These facilities provide high-quality medical care and have English-speaking staff.

Pharmacies: Pharmacies (apoteka) are widely available throughout the city. Many are open late and on weekends, and you can usually find over-the-counter and prescription medications.

Health Insurance

Travel Insurance: It's highly recommended to have comprehensive travel insurance that covers medical emergencies while traveling. Ensure you understand the terms and conditions of your policy.

EHIC: If you are a European Union resident, carry your European Health Insurance Card (EHIC) to access medical services within the EU. However, it may not cover all expenses.

Money and Currency Exchange

Understanding Zagreb's local currency, currency exchange options and payment methods is crucial for a smooth trip. Here's what you need to know:

Currency

The official currency of Croatia is the Croatian Kuna, abbreviated as HRK. Banknotes and coins are commonly used for everyday transactions.

Currency Exchange

Exchange Offices: Currency exchange offices are prevalent throughout Zagreb. Look for authorized and reputable offices to get a fair exchange rate. Avoid exchanging money at hotels, as they may offer less favorable rates.

ATMs: ATMs are widespread in Zagreb and accept major credit and debit cards. Using local ATMs can be an efficient way to withdraw Kuna, but be aware of potential foreign transaction fees from your bank.

Credit Cards

Major credit and debit cards, such as Visa, MasterCard, and American Express, are widely accepted in Zagreb, particularly in hotels, restaurants, and shops. However, carrying some cash for smaller businesses and local markets is advisable.

Communication and Internet

Staying connected while traveling is essential for navigation, communication, and sharing your experiences. Here's what you need to know about communication and internet access in Zagreb:

Mobile Services

SIM Cards: You can purchase prepaid SIM cards from various mobile providers in Zagreb. Some well-known providers include T-Mobile, A1, and Tele2. These SIM cards offer data and calling plans, ensuring you have access to a local number and internet during your Stay.

Roaming: To avoid unexpected fees, check with your mobile provider about international charges and data plans.

Internet Access

Free Wi-Fi: Many hotels, cafes, and public places in Zagreb offer free Wi-Fi access. Look for signs or ask staff for the network name and password.

Internet Cafes: Internet cafes are still available in the city for those who don't have their own devices or need computer access.

Travel Tips and Packing Suggestions

Ensuring a smooth and enjoyable trip to Zagreb involves practical travel tips and packing strategies. Here's a guide to making your visit more comfortable:

Travel Tips

Electrical Adapters: Croatia uses Type C and Type F electrical sockets. Bring the appropriate adapter if your devices have a different plug.

Language: While many people in Zagreb, especially in the service industry, speak English, it's helpful to learn a few basic Croatian phrases and greetings. Locals often appreciate the effort.

Tipping: Tipping is customary in restaurants and cafes. A 10% to 15% tip is usually appreciated for good service.

Local Cuisine: Try local dishes like ćevapi, pastries, and seafood. Croatian wine and rakija (fruit brandy) are also worth exploring.

Respect Cultural Norms: Respect local customs and traditions, and dress modestly when visiting religious sites.

Packing Suggestions

Weather-Appropriate Clothing: Check the weather forecast for your travel dates and pack accordingly. Zagreb experiences four distinct seasons, so bring layers for varying temperatures.

Comfortable Walking Shoes: Zagreb is a walkable city, so comfortable shoes for exploring are necessary.

Travel Adapters: Ensure you have the proper electrical adapters for your devices.

Travel Documents: Keep your passport, travel insurance, and essential documents in a secure, waterproof pouch.

Reusable Water Bottle: Stay hydrated by using a reusable water bottle to refill clean and safe tap water from the city.

In conclusion, understanding and preparing for practical aspects of your trip to Zagreb, from safety and health to currency exchange, communication, and travel tips, will contribute to a more enjoyable and worry-free experience in this beautiful Croatian city. Zagreb is a welcoming and charming destination, and with the correct information and preparation, you'll make the most of your visit.

Chapter 10

Zagreb for Different Travelers

Zagreb, the capital of Croatia, is a diverse and vibrant city that welcomes travelers of all kinds. In this chapter, we'll explore how Zagreb caters to various travelers' unique needs and interests. Whether traveling with your family, on a romantic getaway, exploring solo, identifying as LGBTQ+, or seeking an accessible experience, Zagreb has something unique to offer each group of travelers.

Family-Friendly Zagreb
Zagreb is an excellent destination for families, offering many activities and attractions that will entertain both children and adults. Here's what makes Zagreb family-friendly:

Interactive Museums and Science Centers

Museum of Illusions: Kids will be captivated by the mind-bending exhibits that play with perception and reality. This museum is a fun and educational experience for the whole family.

Zagreb City Museum: Discover the city's history through engaging and interactive displays. Children can explore the past through a series of hands-on exhibits.

Technical Museum Nikola Tesla: Named after the famous inventor, this museum offers a fascinating look at technology and science, making it an ideal destination for curious young minds.

Green Spaces and Parks

Maksimir Park: This sprawling park is a great place for a family picnic, with a zoo that kids will love. You can also rent paddle boats and explore the park's picturesque lakes.

Bundek Lake: Another beautiful park with a lake, Bundek Lake offers playgrounds and walking paths, making it a popular spot for families.

Ice Skating in Winter

During the winter months, the city transforms into a winter wonderland. The ice skating rink in King Tomislav Square is a favorite among families. Rent skates and enjoy gliding across the ice with the backdrop of the city's historic architecture.

Kid-Friendly Dining

Many restaurants in Zagreb are family-friendly and offer children's menus. Try local dishes that appeal to young taste buds, such as "štrukli" (a traditional pastry filled with cheese) or pizza and pasta options.

Family Accommodations

Zagreb provides a range of accommodations suitable for families. You can find hotels with family suites and apartment rentals with multiple bedrooms. Look for accommodations near parks and attractions for added convenience. Remember to check our accommodation chapter in this book.

Romantic Getaways

Zagreb's charm extends to couples seeking a romantic escape. The city's romantic ambiance, picturesque architecture, and cozy nooks make it an ideal destination for lovers. Here are some highlights for a romantic getaway in Zagreb:

Stroll through the Historic Upper Town

Hand in hand, explore the cobblestone streets of Gornji Grad, Zagreb's historic upper town. Wander through St. Mark's Square and soak in the romantic atmosphere.

Candlelit Dinners

Zagreb boasts a thriving culinary scene. Enjoy a romantic dinner at a local restaurant, where you can savor traditional Croatian dishes in a cozy, candlelit setting. Try "štrukli" or fresh seafood dishes for an authentic experience.

Visit the Botanical Gardens

The Botanical Gardens of Zagreb provide a serene environment for couples to stroll amidst lush greenery and vibrant flowers. It's the perfect spot for a quiet escape within the city.

Enjoy a Thermal Spa

For a truly luxurious experience, visit the wellness and thermal spas in and around Zagreb. Soak in thermal baths, get a couple's massage, or relax in a sauna for a day of pampering and rejuvenation.

Watch the Sunset from the Zagreb 360 Observation Deck

For a memorable romantic moment, ascend to the Zagreb 360 Observation Deck in the tallest building in Zagreb. Witness the sun setting over the city for a breathtaking view you'll cherish forever.

Accommodations for Romance

Several boutique hotels in Zagreb offer romantic packages and exceptional amenities, such as in-room champagne and flowers. Consider staying in a historic hotel to add a touch of grandeur to your romantic escape.

Solo Traveler's Guide

Zagreb is a welcoming destination for solo travelers, with its safe streets and a thriving cultural scene. Here are some tips for solo adventurers exploring the city:

Join Guided Walking Tours

One of the best ways to explore Zagreb as a solo traveler is to join guided walking tours. These tours allow one to meet other travelers and learn about the city's history and culture.

Coffee Culture

Zagreb is known for its vibrant cafe culture. Spend your afternoons in local cafes, sipping on a cup of coffee and people-watching. You're likely to strike up conversations with friendly locals and fellow travelers.

Attend Cultural Events

Check the local event calendar for cultural events, concerts, and festivals during your Stay. Attending such events enriches your experience and provides opportunities to connect with people who share your interests.

Explore the Local Art Scene

Zagreb's art galleries and exhibitions offer solo travelers a chance to immerse themselves in the city's creative atmosphere. Take advantage of the opportunity to engage with local artists and art enthusiasts.

Safety and Convenience

Zagreb is known for its safety, making it an excellent choice for solo travelers. Additionally, the city's reliable public transportation system makes it easy to navigate and explore.

Hostel and Social Accommodations

If you're a solo traveler on a budget, consider staying in hostels or guesthouses known for their social atmosphere. You'll find fellow travelers looking to connect and explore the city together.

Accessible Travel

Zagreb is committed to making the city accessible to all travelers, including those with disabilities. Here's how the city caters to accessible travel:

Accessible Transportation

Public transportation in Zagreb is becoming increasingly accessible, with low-floor trams and buses equipped with ramps. Many stations and vehicles are designed to accommodate wheelchair users.

Wheelchair-Friendly Attractions

Zagreb's significant attractions, such as the Cathedral and the Museum of Arts and Crafts, have made efforts to provide wheelchair access and amenities for visitors with disabilities.

Accommodations for All

Several hotels in Zagreb are equipped with accessible rooms and facilities. Check for accommodations that meet your needs, whether you require wheelchair access or other accessible features.

Guided Tours

Some tour operators in Zagreb offer guided tours designed for travelers with disabilities. These tours are carefully crafted to ensure a memorable and accessible experience.

Accessibility in the Outdoors

Zagreb's natural attractions, such as parks and lakes, are increasingly accessible, with paved paths and ramps. The city is working to improve access to outdoor areas for all visitors.

Zagreb's commitment to inclusivity and accessibility ensures that travelers of all backgrounds and abilities can experience the city's rich culture and history. Whether you're visiting as a family, a couple, a solo traveler, part of the LGBTQ+ community, or with accessibility needs, Zagreb has something unique, making it an excellent choice for many travelers.

Conclusion

As your journey through the enchanting city of Zagreb draws to a close, you might find yourself grappling with mixed emotions. Saying goodbye to a place that has embraced you with its warmth, culture, and charm can be bittersweet. The conclusion of your Zagreb adventure is a moment to reflect on the memories you've created, the experiences you've had, and the lasting impressions this Croatian capital left on you. In this final chapter, we'll explore the art of bidding farewell to Zagreb and how to make the most of your last moments in this vibrant city.

Reflecting on Your Zagreb Experience
Before you pack your bags and head to the airport or train station:

Take some time to reflect on your Zagreb journey.

Remember the highlights of your trip, the people you've met, and the places you've explored.

Consider the cultural encounters, delicious dishes, and captivating sights that have become part of your travel story.

One of the best ways to commemorate your journey is to keep a travel journal. Write down your thoughts, feelings, and observations in Zagreb. Capture the essence of each day, the surprises you encountered, and the personal growth you experienced. Your journal can be a cherished memento, allowing you to relive your adventures in Zagreb whenever you wish.

Farewell to Local Friends

If you've had the opportunity to connect with locals during your Stay in Zagreb, saying goodbye can be an emotional experience. These connections can offer you a deeper understanding of the city's culture and make your visit all the more meaningful. Consider inviting your new friends for a farewell meal or coffee to express your gratitude and exchange contact information to stay in touch. Remember that friendships forged during travel often have a special place in your heart.

Last-Minute Explorations

While you may have covered many of Zagreb's must-see attractions during your trip, there might still be a few places or experiences you still need to explore. Your last day in the city can be the perfect opportunity to revisit a favorite spot, enjoy a final meal at a beloved restaurant, or uncover hidden gems you missed. The Upper Town, with its historic charm and panoramic views, is an excellent choice for a stroll.

If you're a lover of souvenirs, Zagreb offers a variety of shops and markets where you can pick up a memento of your visit. Consider visiting Dolac Market to purchase local delicacies like cheese or dried lavender, or browse the Donji Grad (Lower Town) boutiques for unique, handcrafted items.

Taking in Zagreb's Sunset

Watching the sunset in a foreign city is often a breathtaking and reflective experience. Zagreb offers several vantage points to enjoy a serene evening as you bid farewell. The Lotrščak Tower, one of the oldest standing buildings in Zagreb, provides a stunning view of the city at dusk. Additionally, the Zagreb 360 observation deck in the city's heart offers panoramic views of both the Upper and Lower Towns, making it an ideal spot to watch the sun dip below the horizon.

Reliving Memories Through Photography

Photography has a unique way of capturing moments and preserving memories. Before you leave Zagreb, take some final photographs of the city's iconic landmarks, vibrant street scenes, and the people you've met. You'll want to remember the picturesque architecture, the colorful street art, and the everyday moments that make Zagreb unique. These photos will serve as a visual diary of your journey and allow you to share your experiences with friends and family when you return home.

A Last Taste of Zagreb's Cuisine

Croatian cuisine is known for its flavorful dishes, and saying goodbye to Zagreb would only be complete with indulging in one last meal. Whether you dine at a restaurant you've grown fond of or sample a dish you have yet to try, make your farewell dinner in Zagreb memorable.

Don't forget to savor a traditional Croatian dessert, like štrukli, a pastry filled with fresh cheese, or kremsnita, a delightful custard slice. Pair your meal with a glass of local wine or try some rakija, a fruit brandy famous in the region—toast to your unforgettable Zagreb adventure.

Leaving a Positive Impact

As responsible travelers, it's essential to consider the impact of our visits on the places we explore.

Before you say goodbye to Zagreb, ensure you've disposed of any waste properly and respected the environment and local customs. If you've engaged in any activities involving the local community, express your appreciation and respect for the people who welcomed you.

Consider giving back to the community to leave a positive impact. Supporting local artisans by purchasing their products or contributing to a local charity can be a meaningful way to show appreciation for the city and its people.

Departure Logistics

On your departure day, ensure you have all the necessary documents, including your passport, tickets, and travel insurance. Plan your airport or train station transportation in advance, allowing ample time for potential delays. Keep some local currency for any last-minute expenses or emergencies.

Checking in online's a good idea, as it saves time and avoids the hassle of long lines at the airport. Be aware of the baggage weight limits and any airport regulations that may apply to your trip.

Staying Connected

While you may be leaving Zagreb physically, you can still stay connected to the city and its culture. Share your experiences on social media, join online travel forums or groups related to Zagreb, and consider following local accounts to keep up with events and updates from the city.

Additionally, if you've made local friends, maintain those connections through social media or email. This can be a way to stay engaged with Zagreb and potentially plan a return visit in the future.

Farewell, but Not Goodbye
Saying goodbye to Zagreb is undoubtedly a significant moment in your travel experience, but it

doesn't have to be a final farewell. The memories, friendships, and spirit of Zagreb will stay with you long after you've left the city. Consider this goodbye a "see you later" rather than an ending. Keep the possibility of returning to Zagreb in the future alive, as there are always more stories to create and adventures in this remarkable city.

In conclusion, saying goodbye to Zagreb is not just a farewell to a destination; it's a farewell to a part of yourself you've discovered during your journey. The city's rich culture, history, and warm hospitality have left an indelible mark on your heart, making Zagreb a place you'll carry with you forever. Cherish the memories, stay connected, and keep the door open for a future return to this charming Croatian capital. Your adventure in Zagreb may be ending, but the story of your travels is far from over.

Zagreb Travel Journal

Zagreb Travel Journal

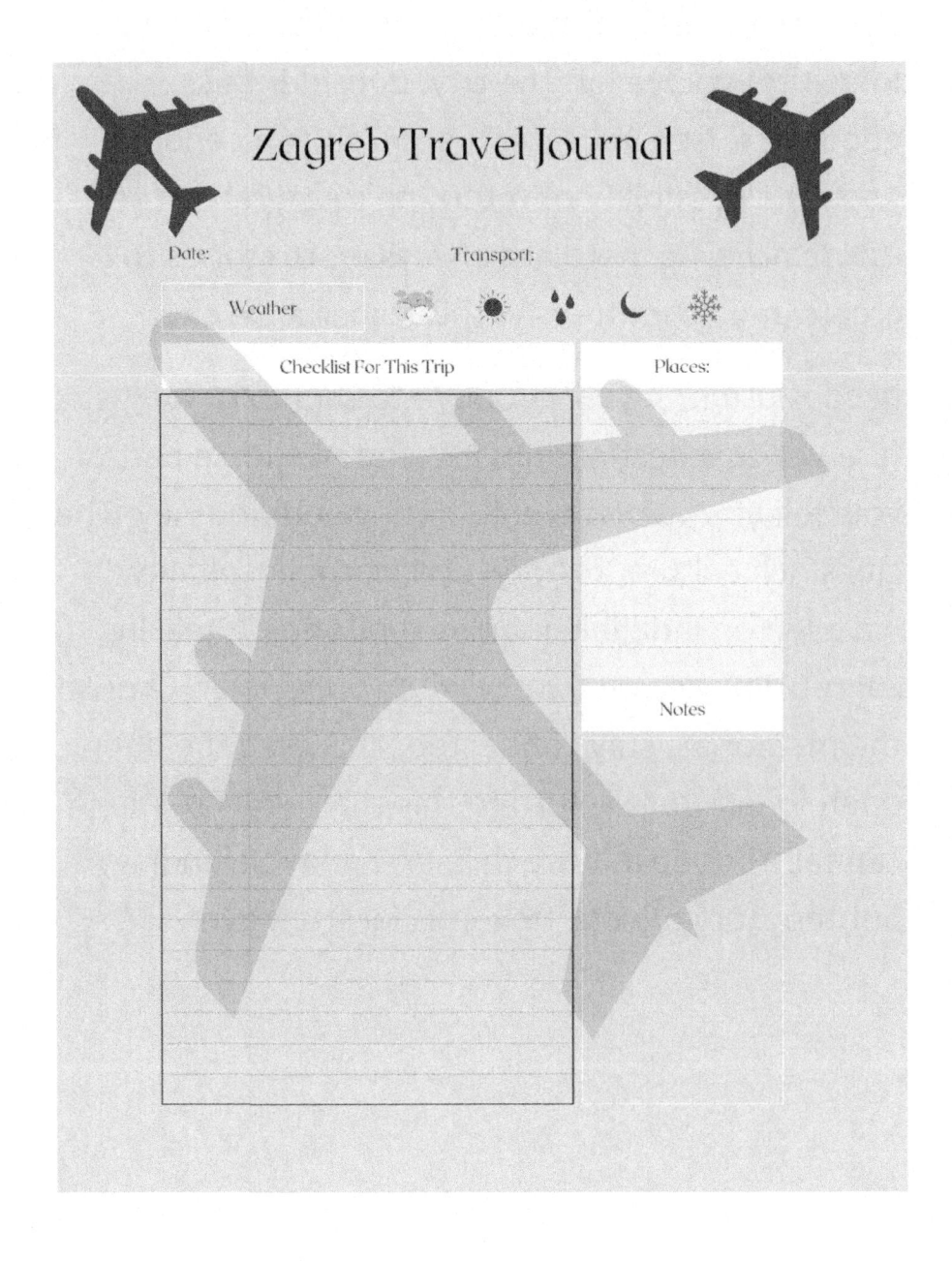

Date: Transport:

Weather

Checklist For This Trip Places:

Notes

Zagreb Travel Journal

Date: _____   Transport: _____

Weather   ☁️ ☀️ 💧 🌙 ❄️

Checklist For This Trip

Places:

Notes

Zagreb Travel Journal

Date: Transport:

Weather

Checklist For This Trip

Places:

Notes

Zagreb Travel Journal

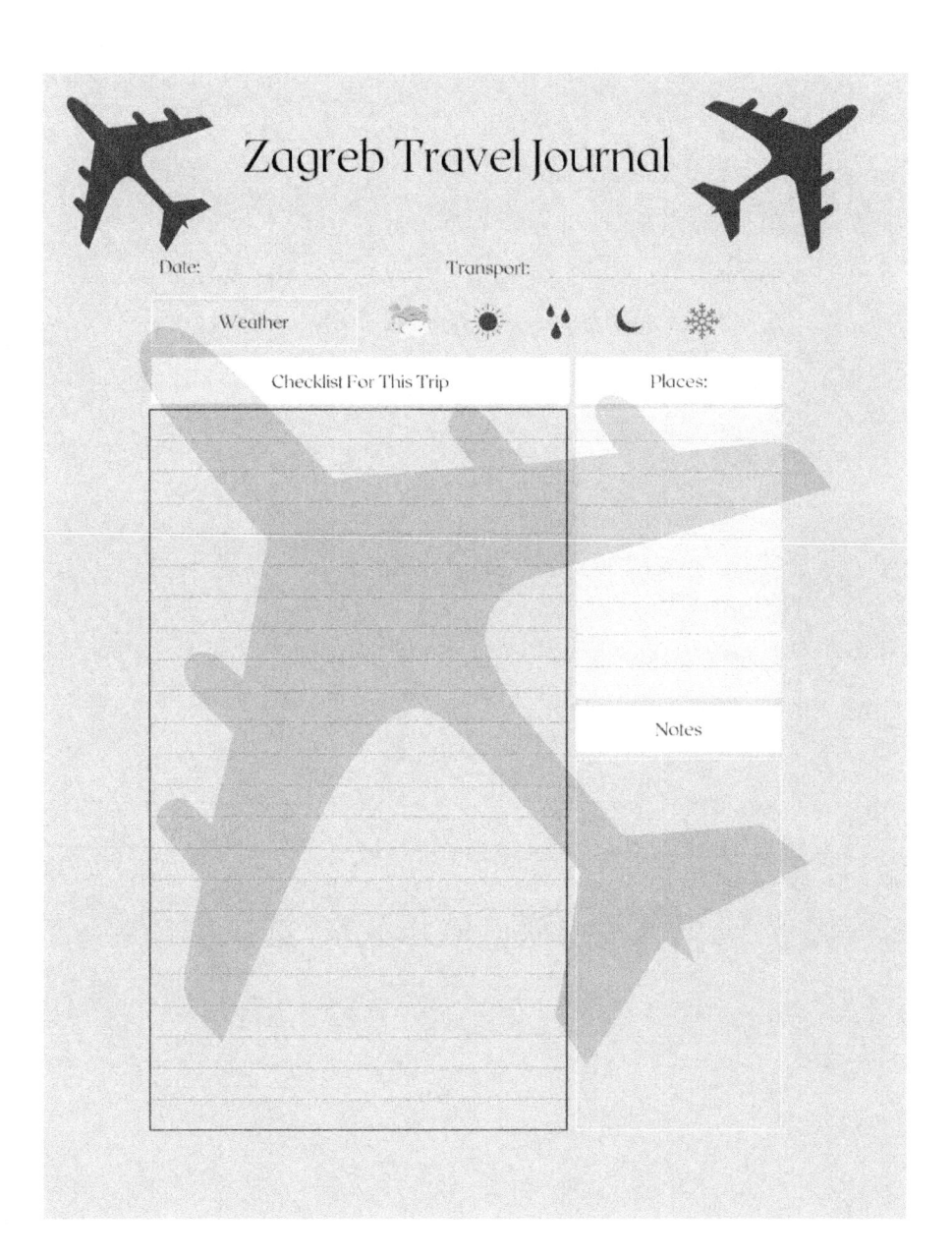

Date: _____ Transport: _____

Weather ☁ ☀ 💧 🌙 ❄

Checklist For This Trip	Places:
	Notes

Zagreb Travel Journal

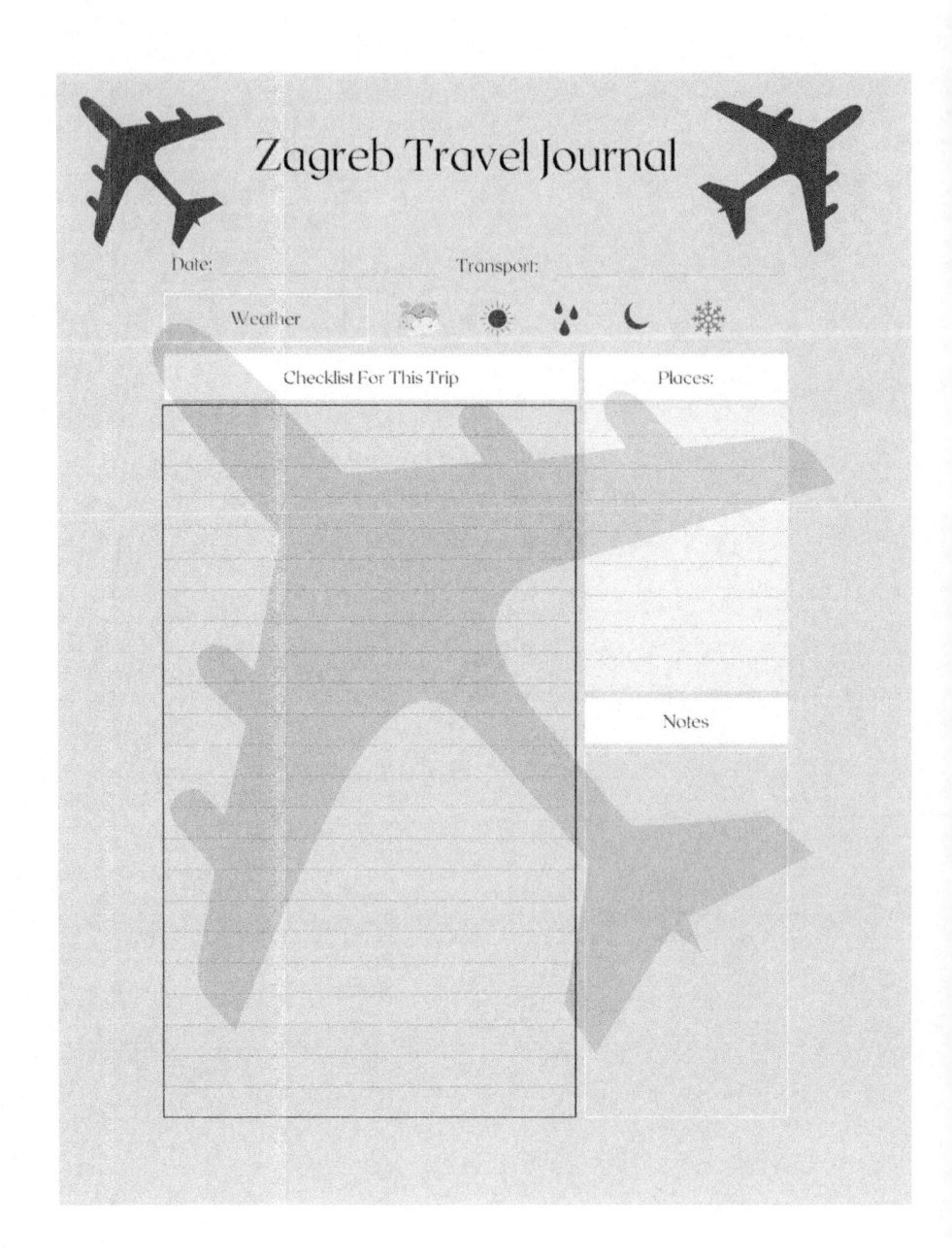

Date: _____ Transport: _____

Weather

Checklist For This Trip

Places:

Notes

Zagreb Travel Journal

Date: _____   Transport: _____

Weather

Checklist For This Trip

Places:

Notes

Zagreb Travel Journal

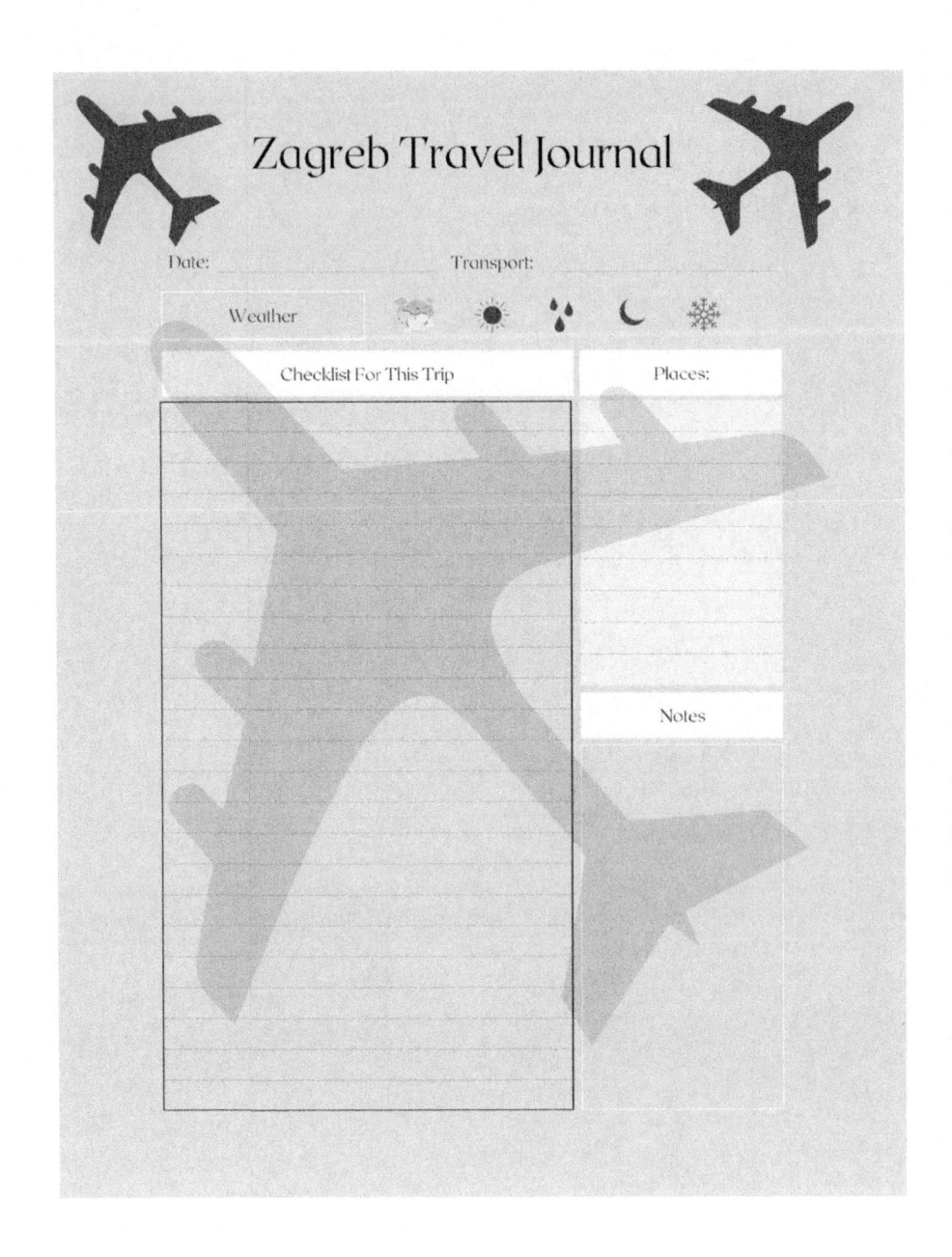

Date: _____   Transport: _____

Weather

Checklist For This Trip

Places:

Notes

Zagreb Travel Journal

Date: _____ Transport: _____

Weather

Checklist For This Trip

Places:

Notes

Zagreb Travel Journal

Date: _____   Transport: _____

Weather:

Checklist For This Trip

Places:

Notes

Zagreb Travel Journal

Date: _____ Transport: _____

Weather: ☁ ☀ 💧 🌙 ❄

Checklist For This Trip

Places:

Notes

Zagreb Travel Journal

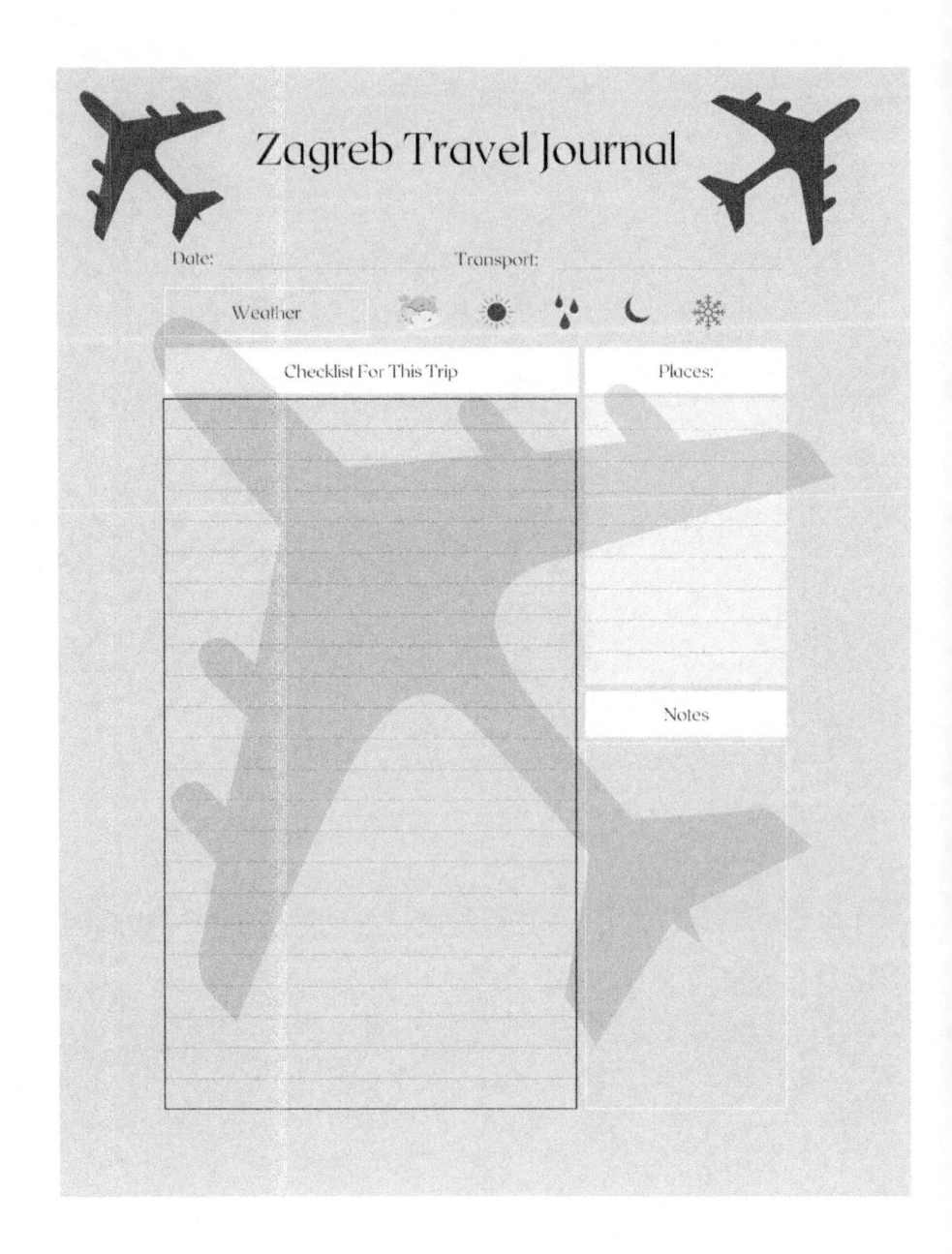

Date: _____   Transport: _____

Weather: 🌥 ☀ 💧 🌙 ❄

Checklist For This Trip	Places:

Notes

Zagreb Travel Journal

Date: _____   Transport: _____

Weather

Checklist For This Trip	Places:

Notes

Zagreb Travel Journal

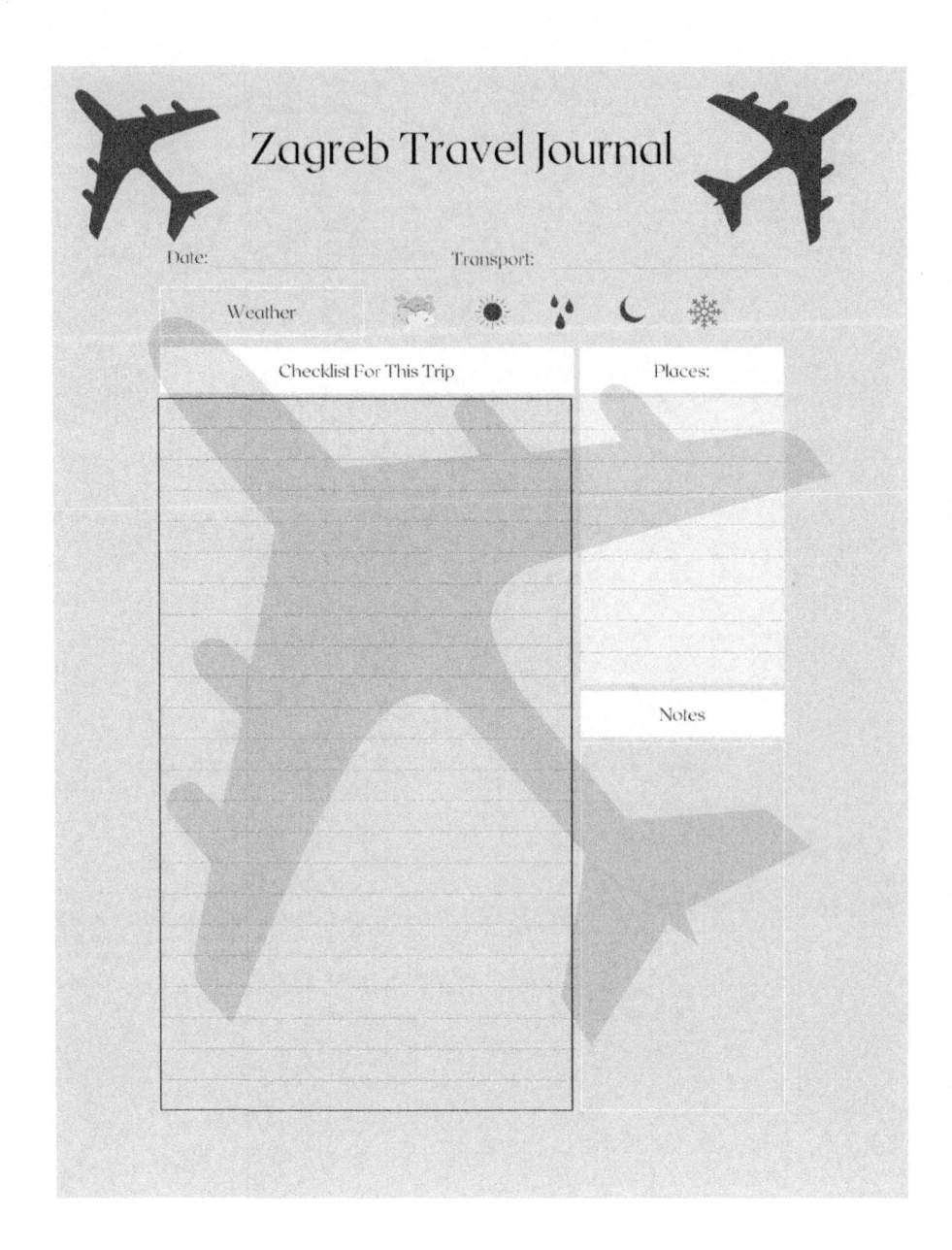

Date: Transport:

Weather

Checklist For This Trip | Places:

Notes

Zagreb Travel Journal

Date: _____ Transport: _____

Weather

Checklist For This Trip

Places:

Notes

Zagreb Travel Journal

Date: _____ Transport: _____

Weather: 🌥 ☀ 💧 ☾ ❄

Checklist For This Trip

Places:

Notes

Zagreb Travel Journal

Date: Transport:

Weather

Checklist For This Trip

Places:

Notes

Zagreb Travel Journal

Date: _____ Transport: _____

Weather

Checklist For This Trip

Places:

Notes

Zagreb Travel Journal

Date: _____ Transport: _____

Weather ☁ ☀ 💧 🌙 ❄

Checklist For This Trip	Places:

Notes

Zagreb Travel Journal

Date: _____ Transport: _____

Weather

Checklist For This Trip | Places:

Notes

Zagreb Travel Journal

Date: _____ Transport: _____

Weather ☁ ☀ 💧 🌙 ❄

Checklist For This Trip

Places:

Notes

Zagreb Travel Journal

Date: _____ Transport: _____

Weather

Checklist For This Trip

Places:

Notes

Zagreb Travel Journal

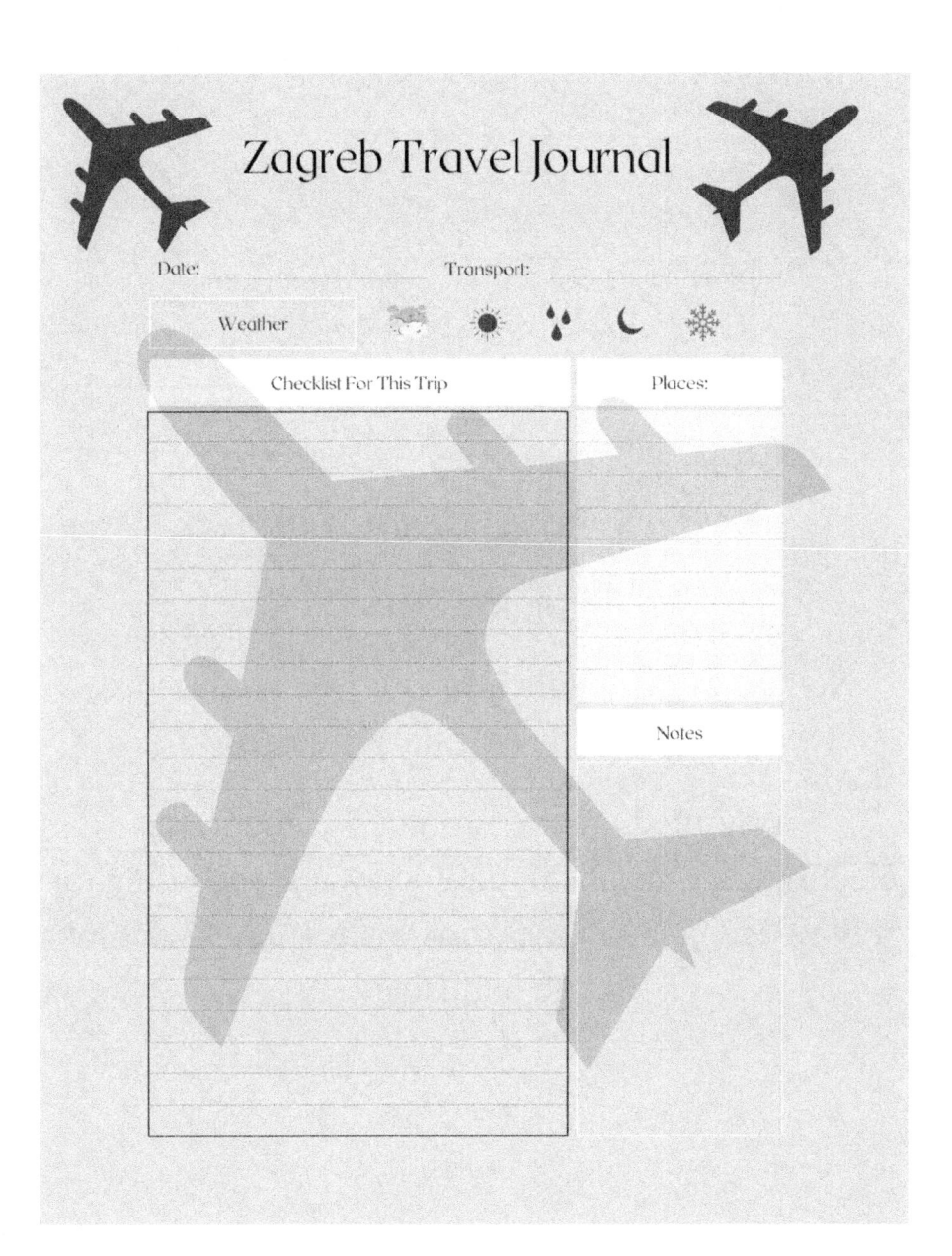

Date: _____ Transport: _____

Weather ☁ ☀ 💧 🌙 ❄

Checklist For This Trip   Places:

Notes

Copyright © 2023 Coast Walker Oz.

All rights reserved.

No part of this publication may be reproduced, stored in a retrieval system, or

transmitted, in any form or by any means, electronic, mechanical, photocopying, recording, or otherwise, without the prior written permission of the publisher.

Printed in Great Britain
by Amazon